COIL OF WISDOM

VOLUME 2
A DAUGHTER'S REFLECTION ON SIGNIFICANCE

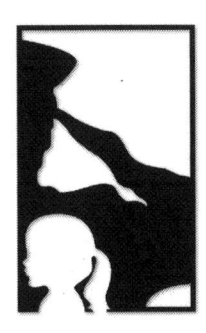

Lauren Ann Schieffer, CSP

LSE Publications
Bonner Springs, KS

Copyright © 2020 by Lauren Ann Schieffer, CSP.
All rights reserved. No part of this publication may be reproduced, distributed or transmitted in any form or by any means, including photocopying, recording, or other electronic or mechanical methods, without the prior written permission of the publisher, except in the case of brief quotations embodied in critical reviews and certain other noncommercial uses permitted by copyright law. For permission requests, write to the publisher, addressed "Attention: Permissions Coordinator," at the address below.
Lauren Ann Schieffer, CSP/LSE Publications
Bonner Springs, KS
www.laurenschieffer.com
Cover design: Mallory Montgomery 2020
Book Layout ©2020 BookDesignTemplates.com
Ordering Information: LS@laurenschieffer.com
Quantity sales. Special discounts are available on quantity purchases by corporations, associations, and others. For details, contact the "Special Sales Department" at the email address above.
Colonels of Wisdom - Significance/ Lauren Ann Schieffer, CSP. —1st ed.
ISBN 978-0-578-68131-3
Photo of father and daughter by Tech. Sgt. Nadine Barclay, courtesy of U.S. Air Force
Photo of saluting airman by Senior Airman Kedesha Pennant, courtesy of U.S. Air Force

What others are saying about
Colonels of Wisdom Vol 2

"These 'colonels' of wisdom give a quick insightful lesson for each week, or all at once. I absolutely love Lauren's ability to take a small quote and give a quick but meaningful story on how to lead, inspire, motivate, and be present in our daily lives. Her reflections inspire us all to be better leaders no matter our place or role. Every time I read or re-read a quote, I am empowered to continue working to better myself and those I encounter in life."

Matt Crouse, Director of Parks and Recreation
City of Nixa, MO

"I never met the Colonel but I feel like I've learned from a selfless leader. Lauren shares so many life lessons her father taught her as a "kiddo." From serving others, to teamwork to purpose over title, ***Colonels of Wisdom, Volume 2*** is timeless and a must read."

Joel Goldberg, Speaker/Broadcaster, Host of *Rounding the Bases*

"In your hands you hold the keys to living a life of true value. At times, it seems that real leaders are rare. In fact, leaders can be found all around us. You too, can be an everyday hero if you read, reflect and practice the principles revealed in this treasure of a book. You may fall from time to time. The good news is you can reset your clock and get back to center in a moment. Keep Lauren's book within arm's reach at all times and refer to it often. The Colonel would be proud!"

Mark LeBlanc, CSP, Author of *Never Be the Same* and *Growing Your Business!*

"Every page of this wonderful new book is filled with the eloquent and profound wisdom of "the Colonel" (aka author Lauren Schieffer's father). Fortunately, Schieffer not only remembers these 52 life lessons, but has also chosen to share them with us. While I could summarize the Colonel's philosophy in two words — "Choose Significance" — it would be doing you a disservice. You owe it to yourself to devour and digest this book the same way I did: from cover to cover."

Bill Stainton, CSP, CPAE - 29-time Emmy Winner and Hall of Fame Speaker, Author of *The Five Best Decisions the Beatles Ever Made*

"Significance doesn't come from power. It comes from Value. This book shows you how to truly be of value to others. It shows you through simple daily guidance how to reframe your thinking and therefore shape your actions to make a difference.

Read it often, not just once like a novel, but daily so that the Colonel's Wisdom can guide you as it has others."

Jim Cathcart, Professional Mentor, author of *The Power Minute*

"52 wonderful gems of inspiration offered in love by a father to a daughter and shared with us by her. What a great tool this book is to guide you through a year of productivity, service and significance. Each week's quote builds a stronger foundation for a better you."

Wayne Schoeneberg, Attorney, Speaker, Author of *No Clients? No Job? No Problem!* And *Dominate Your Divorce*

"I thought this would be just another quote book. It is so much more! It's meaningful wisdom a loving dad offered to his daughter, that she has graciously shared with us. Lauren's messages that follow each quote are powerful, poignant and applicable for all of us as we journey through life trying to be significant and make a difference. Everyone should read this simple and significant book full of treasures and tools to live an exceptional life."

Annie Meehan, Speaker, Author of *Be the Exception* and *The Pineapple Principle*

"*Colonels of Wisdom Vol 2 - A Daughter's Reflection on Significance* shows Lauren's amazing ability to connect others through storytelling. This book will influence and inspire you to refocus as individuals and leaders in today's complex world."

Lori Maher-McCombs, President, The Maher Group Association Management & Event Professional

"You don't just read this book; you go on a journey with it. Each page contains wisdom and insight we can use to help guide us on this journey we call life. When you finish reading it the first time you will realize there is more to learn and you will read the book a second and third time."

Mark Hunter CSP, "The Sales Hunter," Author of *High Profit Prospecting* and *A Mind for Sales*

"What I love about Lauren's writing is the practical advice from the Colonel. As I read it, I can hear my own Dad's voice in my head giving me similar words. Advice from a father to a daughter is important and so are the lessons in this book."

Laurie Guest, CSP - Professional Speaker and Trainer, Author of *The 10¢ Decision: How Small Changes Pays Off Big*

"This is a must-read for every leader and potential leader. Lauren Schieffer's excellence in storytelling provides insight and inspiration on every page. The lessons learned are invaluable in business and in life. This book is ideal for a dose of weekly inspiration (52 'colonels' of wisdom), or to read from cover to cover. Team leaders might also consider utilizing it this year for a weekly lesson with discussion during staff meetings. Thank you, Lauren for providing a true road map to lifetime success and happiness."

Marianne Roesler, Leadership Mentor and Training Consultant

"Just finished reading, *Colonels of Wisdom Vol 2 – A Daughter's Reflection on Significance* in one sitting. It is a fun and entertaining read which offers 52 core concepts the reader can follow to lead a life of significance. I highly recommend using this book as a study-guide to becoming a better person over the course of one year. The world needs more leaders like Lauren Schieffer!"

Earl Bell, Author, *Winning in Baseball and Business*

"There are many books out there that speak to success, but few books that speak to character. And what is success without character? I have been a fan of Lauren Schieffer from the stage. So happy to now have her wisdom in this book I will share with my son. This book should be on EVERY shelf inside and outside the office."

Kelly C Swanson, Speaker, Comedienne, Star of *Who Hijacked My Fairytale?*

For Ruth Ann
5/11/37 – 7/14/19
Mother, Friend, Free-Spirit
who visited me in a dream after she passed,
and said, "Quit dawdling, Lauren Ann,
and finish the damn book!"

Introduction

My father was a Lieutenant Colonel in the U.S. Air Force, and as is the case with most, if not all, fathers, he had been a primary influence on my life and the person I grew to be. To say I was a bit adrift after his death is an understatement. I would hear his voice in the back of my head so often during those first few months, and sadly, I could not help but focus on the reality that I would not hear that voice again. That was the impetus for me to begin writing down the things my father told me. It helped to ground me during that first year and became part of my grieving process.

My first book, *Road Signs on the High Road of Life*, grew out of the eulogy I gave at his memorial and stands on its own as a collection of life lessons. But as time went on, I realized there were so many other things I needed to remember, and so I began to collect them in a single document. I called them "Colonelisms." As my collection grew, I realized they were naturally grouped into a few categories: leadership – what it means to be a leader; significance – how to live a life of impact and influence; and accountability – self-discipline and responsibility.

I had originally thought to simply turn this collection over to my children so they could better remember their "Grandpa Ho Ho," so I was a bit taken aback when a colleague asked if he could have a copy of my collection. Within a month, three other people made the same request. That's when I decided I needed to publish Dad's wisdom.

That is how this trilogy formulated. I have decided to publish this in three volumes, as the three categories revealed themselves to me: Leadership, Significance and Accountability. These three concepts go a long way toward defining who The Colonel was and what he tried to teach me. I have narrowed each category down to fifty-two quotes so they can be utilized as a year-long study—one per week—if desired.

The first in the series, ***Colonels of Wisdom Vol 1 – A Daughter's Reflection on Leadership***, was published in 2018, and I am happy to offer the second volume to you now. The third is still in outline form, so look for it soon.

I have offered insights in this book on what each of these quotes mean to me and how they can be applied in life and business. That doesn't mean these are the only correct interpretations of my father's wisdom; they are simply mine.

I have specifically written these quotes and Dad's words as I remember my father saying them. That means the grammar is not always perfect, and they are peppered with many "kid's," "kiddo's," "young lady's," and other addresses my dad used when he spoke to me. I hope you will indulge me in that and read the wisdom through it. There is a lot to be learned from The Colonel. I hope you get as much out of it as he would have hoped.

Colonels of Wisdom - Significance

This is my absolute favorite picture of my dad. Taken up at our cabin in 1969. I am tucked safely under his arm and, as always, he is working (note the pen in his hand and the pad in his lap). This picture more than any other defines our relationship.

1.

"Anyone can be successful, kiddo. Making a lot of money, that's easy. Choose to be significant."

I start here because this was the greatest challenge The Colonel issued to his daughters. It was what he considered the ultimate measure of a person's life. You see, **significance** has nothing whatsoever to do with how much money you make, what your title is, or how much power you perceive yourself to have. All of those are the way people measure **success**. Significance, on the other hand, is a measure of how many lives you touch and the manner in which you choose to impact them—because how you affect someone's life is a *choice*. You can choose to have a positive impact on others, or you can choose to focus on yourself entirely, which can lead to a negative impact or no impact at all.

So, if we always endeavor to pursue a positive impact, what might that look like and how might we accomplish it? Through his example, without consciously knowing it, The Colonel gifted me with a loose and unofficial list of ideas. These are questions you might ask yourself regularly:

- Have I given without expectation of receiving?
- Who have I mentored, taught, coached, or helped in some way?
- Have I relinquished an opportunity because I knew it would have a more powerful impact if given to someone else?
- Have I spent time with someone simply because I knew they were lonely and needed someone to talk to who would genuinely listen?
- What have I done to make my immediate community a better place?
- Have I given truly and entirely anonymously?
- Have I been there for friends and family even when it was less than convenient to do so?
- Have I shown compassion to everyone I encounter?

I understand this is a weighty list, and no one could be expected to achieve all of these things every day. Some days we fall short entirely, but endeavoring to tick off one each day is an excellent start.

The Colonel was highly driven, but not specifically toward financial wealth. He pushed his daughters to be exceptional, which is both a good aspiration and a heavy burden to bear as a kid. I remember once, early in my marriage, ranting irrationally at my husband about something he said was "fine." I said, "What is 'fine'? Fine is average. Fine is adequate. I'd rather be dead than adequate!" I fully admit that was irrational and born out of an innate need to excel. Nowadays, I calibrate more closely with Dad's challenge to be significant and channel that drive to benefitting others whenever I can. Focusing on that brings me success as well, I have discovered, and frees me from that complex relationship with excellence.

I encourage you to join me in this quest to benefit others first, because anyone can be successful. Choose to be significant instead.

Colonels of Wisdom - Significance

2.

"Your value doesn't have to be earned or bought, kiddo. Your value is inherent because you exist. It just IS."

In the 21st century, many people base their value upon their net worth or the title they hold. Unfortunately, such measurements are fleeting. Your value does not rest in who your parents are, who you're married to or dating, how much money you have, or what your title is. Your value is not determined by what size you wear, what kind of car you drive, whose name is stitched into the collar of your clothes or on your shoes, what color your skin or hair is, what color your eyes are, or how fit, svelte or sexually attractive you are. None of the things that society utilizes to assign value matter at all. Your value rests solely in the fact that you exist and are, therefore, worthy of merit.

The challenge is that unless this self-esteem is instilled in you by your parents (and few people are that lucky), it's a tough concept to grasp, especially in today's skin-deep society. Once grasped, it's even harder to maintain. But I believe very strongly that if you don't love yourself—as you are—it is impossible to love others as they are, which makes it impossible to have a servant's heart.

I know this is hard because it's something that I struggle with often. I did not discover that I had value separate from being my father's daughter until well into my twenties. As child development goes, that's pretty late to develop self-esteem. Therefore, I have to work hard at it every day, even now.

Here are some strategies that have helped me and that I utilize consistently. First, never compare yourself with anyone else. To do so is destructive; we never win that comparison and therefore feel worse about ourselves.

Secondly, associate with positive people. Inherently negative people tend to bring those around them down as well. You will become like the five people you spend the most time around, so why would you choose to spend time around negative people? The more time you spend around those who see the sunshine through the clouds and naturally lift others up, the easier it will be to see yourself through their eyes.

Thirdly, keep a journal of things that are wonderful about you and that you did well. When someone else says something complimentary about you, write it down in your journal, rather than brushing it off. Write in it every day. This gives you something to refer to when you're feeling down about yourself.

Finally, and most importantly, speak only positive thoughts to yourself. Your subconscious mind is three times as strong as your conscious mind. It takes everything it hears as fact and sets about making it truth to you. So, when you say negative things to yourself, which we all do all the time, your subconscious mind solidifies that statement as truth. Instead of saying, "Geez, I'm so clumsy," when you fall, consider saying, "That's not like me. I'm not clumsy." I sincerely believe if you change what you say when you talk to yourself, you can change your life.

Just like maintaining your physical fitness requires discipline—eating well, drinking lots of water, and exercising regularly—your self-esteem is part of your emotional fitness. Maintaining it is just as much a discipline that requires consistent effort.

Remember that you have value—because you exist. Your worth is not affected by anything outside of you. It just IS.

3.

"Blowing out someone else's candle won't make yours shine any brighter, kiddo."

It's important to understand that there is a difference between self-confidence and self-esteem. Self-confidence tells you that you can do a particular task well. It tells you that you are capable. Self-esteem, on the other hand, tells you that you have value because you exist and are therefore worthy of merit. Furthermore, self-esteem tells you that no outside force can erode this inherent value.

Truly understanding that your value is inherent, that it doesn't have to be earned and can't be purchased, does not make you boastful or conceited. On the contrary, that knowledge frees you to be humble. Most arrogant people I've met have little or no self-esteem. If you take the biggest bully you can think of and crack them open like an egg, down in the center you will find a tiny child with no self-esteem. They have just protected themselves with layers and layers of arrogance as a defense mechanism.

We have all met people who put others down to make themselves look or feel bigger and better. They gather for themselves a false sense of self-esteem, sort of like picking up the chaff from a threshing floor, after they have knocked someone down or stomped on their hearts or dreams. Unfortunately, their satisfaction is fleeting because it's not rooted in any foundation within themselves. Eventually, they have to find another target to belittle, and they root around the metaphorical threshing floor again and again.

Many people I've met who have a habit of belittling or bullying others do so because they were themselves belittled and never developed any coping skills. If you are continually fed the message that you aren't good enough, aren't strong enough, aren't smart enough, aren't rich enough, or have to be better than others to have any value, it's normal and natural to manifest that message by being a bully. All empathy for them aside, let me be very clear. Belittling someone else does not make you any bigger or any better. It makes you appear smaller and less significant.

If you have people like that in your life, at work, or in your community, you will not be able to change them. It is, I believe, a futile waste of energy. Your energy is better spent leading by example and bolstering those who have been stepped on or put down.

Using Dad's analogy, if I blow out someone else's candle, mine does not get any brighter. The only result is the entire space gets dimmer and darker. My candle has to do all the work. On the other hand, if I use my candle to support or ignite someone else's candle, mine does not diminish at all. The entire space becomes brighter, and the light is stronger for it. My candle has to do less work as it is part of a community of strong lights. What would the world look like if we all focused on supporting and igniting just one other candle?

Colonels of Wisdom - Significance

4.

"Everyone wants to feel like they belong to something bigger than themselves. It gives them a purpose and the ability to feel useful."

One of the base needs of human nature is the need to be included. We want to be encouraged and valued by a greater whole. We were created to be in community. We are stronger in community. That natural tendency doesn't disappear when we step into our careers. Even solopreneurs join associations, co-ops, and mastermind groups to share their insights, seek guidance, and receive validation.

A friend of mine, who is also a former pastor, once said in jest, "If you want to get a congregation moving and serving, go into debt and take on a big capital project." When there is a shared vision and everyone understands it can't be accomplished without each person's effort, amazing things happen. Our nation has rarely come together in a manner that is even close to the communal effort that occurred during WWII, with everyone making sacrifices for the war effort and supporting each other emotionally. The only thing that has come close since then is the sense of community felt immediately following the attacks of 9-11-01.

You see, when people come together to address a big challenge—bigger than anyone can handle alone—leaders emerge, new talents are discovered, and everyone finds their role.

The Colonel's time in the Air Force was entirely a collaboration in support of a more significant cause. Early in his career, he designed buildings that would withstand bombing raids and bombs that would have the maximum effect on a target with minimal impact on the surrounding area. Later as Division Chief of the Flight Dynamics Laboratory, his staff designed the advanced composite materials that the stealth bombers and F-series fighters are constructed with. His career was wholly focused on leading teams toward results that would make those deployed in harm's way more accurate, more effective, and safer, so they could come home to their families. That was a pretty big cause, and he made sure each member of his staff knew how important their work was. He was a master at inclusion. No matter rank, age, or gender, there was a place for you in his action plan.

He infused those experiences into the way he raised his family. We were a team, each one of us with a distinct purpose. We always felt that our contribution was vital. Little girls can't lift a crank-shaft, but we could be ready to hand our Daddy a tool when he needed it while he tinkered with the car. That job was important. He couldn't do it without us (or so I thought at the time).

You can be successful alone, with an entirely solo effort, but you will not be significant that way. Being significant requires community. It requires understanding the universal need everyone has to *belong*, finding a way to create community, and allowing everyone to find their role in that community.

5.

"Significance isn't about you, kid. Focus on how your achievements will help others, and then you'll begin to be significant."

"As I discussed in the first volume, *Reflections on Leadership*, I've spent twenty years as a Mary Kay consultant or director, which was a valuable learning experience for me in many ways. During my time as a consultant, I attended many national conventions. As I sat in the nosebleed seats at my first convention, I was green with envy as my idols walked the stage, receiving beautiful pieces of jewelry in recognition of their promotions and specific business achievements. Their beaming faces flashed on the jumbo screens, and the entire company cheered as each person enjoyed their moment.

Afterward, in recounting the experience to my Dad, I said, "Mark my words, that'll be me in two years. I'm going to start picking out my dress now."

"Maybe," he said, "but if that's all you want, you're thinking pretty shallow."

He could see the disappointment in my face. That was not the response I was looking for. "Look, kiddo," he went on, "if all you want is to look amazing in a fancy dress while you walk across the stage and have people cheer for you, then that's fine. But I think there is so much more to that moment than you're getting."

He reminded me that none of those accolades were achieved alone. Each of those winners had teams. Those teams were made up of women who came from all walks of life and who had all personality types. Their leader showed them how to achieve—how to become more than they previously thought they could be. Their leader encouraged them, sacrificed for them, stayed up late, got up early, told them the truth when it was hard, and traveled untold miles to model for them what a leader looks like. Those in the audience cheering understood that. They realized what a significant, servant leader looked like and what it took to get there. "It's not about the dress, kiddo. It's about helping others achieve *their* special dream. You will know you've been significant when people who talk about you don't talk about what you accomplished for yourself, but rather what you've achieved in the service of others."

6.

"You can offer a service, or you can be willing to serve. There's a difference. Oh, you might get paid for both, but only one is generous, and only one will build significance."

Colonels of Wisdom - Significance

When I was a little girl, Dad and I would often take Sunday afternoon walks on base. Sometimes we'd stop at the ice cream counter in the Base Exchange for ice cream cones. I looked forward to ordering my favorite flavor, mint chocolate chip. The teens behind the counter, wearing their crisp blue uniform hats, looked so grown up to me.

One day, as the young lady serving us handed me my cone, Dad cautioned me to keep it level, so it didn't tip over too far. Of course, I was not paying attention, and before I knew it, the top scoop of my ice cream cone seemed to jump off and dive for the black and white checkered floor. I immediately dissolved into tears. I thought Dad would be mad at me. He had told me to pay attention. He'd paid for that ice cream. I had wasted it *and* made a mess on the floor.

The bright-eyed teenager behind the register jumped into action, darting out in front of the counter and apologizing. She quickly cleaned up the sloppy green mess, all the while trying to comfort me and assure me it was *her* fault. She hadn't pressed the top scoop down strongly enough. Then she ran back around the case and prepared an extra-large double scoop for me. "No charge," she told Dad.

Dad smiled, tipped the girl, and made sure to mention her kindness to the manager (leaving out the free ice cream just in case it would get her in trouble).

That teenager grasped the essence of being willing to serve. Not only did she make a little girl happy, but she also solidified that we would always come back to that special ice cream shop. Although I don't know for sure, I choose to believe that she is leading a major corporation now, using her servant's heart to lead others well. I know I will never forget her.

Colonels of Wisdom - Significance

7.

"Whether it's time or money, kiddo, don't give to get. Give to offer a benefit. Be generous, expecting nothing in return."

Recently, I was sitting in an audience listening to a genuinely exceptional colleague. He is an accomplished keynote speaker who was presenting a session at an event where I was also scheduled to present. He knocked it out of the park, and I knew the audience would be lining up to meet him and request a signed book. I also knew that he had no assistant with him and wouldn't be able to be fully present for each fan who wanted his attention.

During the applause following his keynote, I hopped up to the table at the back of the room, where his stack of books was ready for signing and purchase. When he made his way over, he was surprised to see me sitting there, as we hadn't ever officially met. I introduced myself as a fellow professional speaker from another state chapter and asked for his credit card machine.

"I don't have one," he replied, somewhat confused.

"So, we're taking cash and checks and writing down numbers? Ok. I'll handle the money. You go ahead—sign, schmooze, and be brilliant."

"Lauren, can I take you with me everywhere?"

Now, I don't share this story to boast about the fantastic help I offered him that day. I tell it because it is an example of a small act of kindness that was much appreciated. It cost me nothing, but it may have allowed him to book more future business and make valuable connections in that golden moment after a speech. I know what it feels like to be stuck behind the table, taking information, when the CEO of the dream client company waits over in the corner, and I can't get to her! I helped alleviate that situation for him that day.

I may never see him again. Helping him out that day may never reap any rewards for my business, but it was the right thing to do at the moment. (And it did feel pretty good to be helping out a colleague, which is ok too!)

8.

"Keep on keeping on, kid. Significance doesn't grow out of one attempt. Significance comes from pushing through countless failed attempts and still keeping at it. That's the only way you learn."

Long before Dad took charge of the Flight Dynamics Laboratory, he was playing with airplanes. When I was eight years old, Dad spent countless hours and an "obscene amount of money" (my mother's words; probably about $200 in those days) to construct a remote-control model airplane. Remote control (or "radio-controlled" as they were called then) cars and planes were a brand-new technology at the time, and this thing was massive. It had a six-foot wingspan and took up all of the space in the garage during the year Dad spent building it.

I remember the enthusiasm and anticipation that fall morning when we all piled into the Jeep with the plane in a flatbed trailer behind us and headed out to the mesa south of Chandler, AZ, to test "the bird" on her maiden voyage. Of course, it took a good hour to get everything ready. Dad had to make sure the receivers were working and set the cameras (both still and 8mm) to record the event. Finally, everything was ready.

"Here goes nothing," he said as he fired up the plane's propeller. He slowly pushed the throttle lever, and the model started rolling down the make-shift runway. Before we could blink, the bird was in the air and flying!

And flying... And flying...

"Are you gonna turn it around before it's out of range?" Mom asked apprehensively as we watched it get smaller and smaller in the distance. "Um, I'm not quite sure I how to do that. I didn't think that far. I didn't think she would actually fly today." So, there we all stood watching a year of Dad's life and $200 fly off into the sunset, never to be seen again. Oh, we drove off across the mesa looking for it until it got dark, but we never actually found the bird.

Although Mom didn't let Dad forget that first, lost "toy" for a *very* long time, the lessons we learned from that costly mistake were invaluable. We learned those things we don't anticipate are the very things that will go wrong. We learned to always have a back-up plan. We learned to expect the unexpected—and Dad learned to never again tell Mom how much he had spent on his many and varied projects!

Dad's initial R.C. plane debacle did not keep him from building a second and many more after that. He kept at it, always looking for ways to improve the design. With each new model, he would adapt the wing structure or sculpt his own airfoils for the wings. He tried hundreds of different materials and combinations. Some worked well, some didn't, but each iteration taught him things he would then put into play as he and his team designed new materials and new structures for planes used by the Air Force. That tenacity manifested itself in planes that are still in the air today.

9.

"Focus on getting rich, and you will make money. Focus on making a difference, and who knows—you just might change the world."

The word "rich" is a button pusher for me. How do you know when you are "rich"? How much wealth is required to assign yourself that title? I have observed many people with obscene wealth (by anyone's standards) who are still obsessed with obtaining more. I have also seen people with great wealth who focus on using it to benefit others.

In The Colonel's household, the emphasis was placed on becoming a well-rounded person and being able to give back, rather than on the pursuit of wealth. We were expected to support ourselves as adults and also be ready to serve those around us who could benefit from our help.

Once, when we were stationed at Kirtland AFB, Dad met a young man who needed a car to get to work so he could support his family. Dad knew this kid had no money—and Dad happened to have a vehicle that he was planning to sell. (Dad always had a spare-parts car around.) He could have sold the car to someone else for at least a thousand dollars and was planning on using those funds to build his shed and workroom in the backyard. In Dad's mind, it came down to this question: Did he need the shed more than this young man needed the car? What decision was going to make a more significant difference in someone's life?

Dad gave him the car.

We were never rich by anyone's financial standards. Nothing we had was ever new, shiny, or glamorous. We did okay, and we got by. The Colonel believed that riches come in the form of talents, skills, wisdom, health, and stamina. These are the riches beyond price—the gifts we are given by God and the universe. He believed that those were the riches we needed to gather and use to make a difference.

What "riches" are you focused on gathering? There is nothing wrong with accumulating financial wealth. A lot of good can be accomplished with wealth. The question simply becomes, what difference are you making with the riches that you are accumulating?

10.

"Know why you get up every day and go to work, kid. Then, when it gets tough, your WHY will keep you from hitting the snooze again."

In the network marketing world, new consultants are often coached to "find their big *Why.*" In other words, find that which is universally relevant but specifically valid only for you. Your "*Why*" (with a capital W) is what powers and propels you (uniquely and relentlessly) toward your goal. It's what gets you up in the morning and what keeps you going when you get discouraged or feel like quitting.

The Colonel taught me about this well before it became a mainstream concept. He believed that you have to work "dang hard" to make it in this world, so you better 1) be sure you pick something you enjoy working at and 2) know *why* you are working so hard at it. As I began looking at choices for a profession, Dad reminded me that the decisions I made should involve more than seeking the highest paying job. They should be about finding "my calling."

Mary Kay Ash told her beauty consultants to find something you enjoy so much you would do it for free, and the joy you bring to it will naturally attract people who will pay you to do it.

One of the legends in the Arbonne organization often says, "Money isn't everything, but it's right up there with oxygen. And I think we should have as much of both as we want. Follow your why, and the money will follow you." Another millionaire entrepreneur says, "Money doesn't buy happiness. Money buys choices. The choices you make as a result of the money is what is either fulfilling or not."

While such paradigms are fun and perhaps comforting to hear, they are most often not the typical progression of thought. Most people follow the money trail. They look for the next big promotion with the healthy raise and assume that is what's going to make them happy. Indeed, profit may come as a result of being good at what you do, but unfortunately, I know a great many people making a lot of money and hating every minute of what they are doing so well.

On the other hand, if we are striving for significance, it only comes as a result of why we are doing what we are doing. Unless that next promotion fulfills your *"Why,"* you may find yourself unfulfilled and therefore hitting that snooze button every morning.

11.

"If you know where you're going and WHY you're going there, it won't matter how or when you get there."

Vision boards are all the rage in direct sales. Vision boards are a tool that team leaders often use to inspire their followers to imagine what their life will look like once they reach a particular level of achievement. Magazine photos of sunny vacation destinations, dream homes, even cash falling from the sky show up on foam-core boards at team retreats throughout organizations across the globe, regardless of the product or company. As a Mary Kay Sales Director, I began every new Seminar Year with my unit by making vision boards for what they wanted to accomplish in the upcoming year and beyond.

Please don't misunderstand me. I do believe in the power of visualization. I believe in invoking all our senses to create the life we desire before it happens. The challenge with this visioning exercise is that it's too often conducted with only the end in mind. It's all about where you're going and by when. There is rarely anything about WHY you are going there, which is the reason the same goals and life-vision so often end up on a person's board every year, unattained. As I mentioned in the previous section, the *why* is the most vital piece of the puzzle! It's so much more important than the what, where, or when.

You see, there are whys with a small w, like "Why do I go to work? To get paid so I can pay my bills. That's why I go to work." But there are also WHYs in all caps. These are larger, umbrella WHYs that affect your significance and ability to stick with the vision when the seas of life get rough. Maybe you are working extra shifts and taking those specific wages to donate to the orphanage in Uganda that you visited while you were on a mission trip there. Maybe you're building a work-from-home business so you can be the primary caregiver for your spouse who is suffering from cancer. These types of things are the all-caps WHYs.

In your career, if you don't know why you are showing up, it's all too easy to let small, petty setbacks get in the way. It's all too easy to not show up at all. Dad pushed his daughters to always look to the WHY and only reset the time frame as necessary.

If you know the big WHY, then when you encounter obstacles and have to adjust the when, you don't go off track. When you can't be stopped from pursuing the big WHY, even if how you or when you achieve it change, you know for certain that you *will* achieve it.

Colonels of Wisdom - Significance

12.

"Allow yourself to shine, kid. Don't spend so much time 'looking for the light' that you forget you can be light."

Sometimes I think Dad struggled, wondering what to do with two daughters. It might have been easier for him if he'd had sons to teach and mentor. Yet, everything he might have taught sons—engineering, football, healthy competition, leadership, how to change a tire or the oil in a car—he went ahead and taught his daughters.

One of the things he could not understand, for the life of him, is *why* on earth his daughters might shrink from taking the lead on a project or pretend to be less intelligent than we were. It was (and unfortunately probably still is) common in middle school and high school for girls to "dumb down," thinking that this will make them less intimidating or more attractive to teenage boys. My sister and I were no different, although both of us snapped out of it pretty quickly after high school. The whole concept completely baffled and frustrated my father.

Sometimes we are hesitant to step up and step out into the spotlight for fear of what others will think of us. Will I be perceived as too pushy? Am I too boastful? There is a quote I love, which is attributed to the wise sage "Grandma," that says, "Someone else's opinion of you is none of your business." I love that, and Dad would have too.

You can't be significant if you refuse to allow your light to shine. Perhaps if you are willing to shine, you'll inspire others to step into their light and share a gift that will move their team or community forward. No one would consciously hold someone else back from achieving their greatness. Yet, if we hold ourselves back, then perhaps the inspiration is not there for others to see and build upon. Each of us has unique gifts given to us for a reason. Use them. Don't be afraid to inspire others. Be willing to be the light.

Colonels of Wisdom - Significance

13.

"Look, we're all going to die at some point, kid. That's not a choice.

How you choose to live... that is your call. Choose to live full out."

Do you remember being a little boy or girl and stomping through mud puddles? Do you remember jumping on the playground swings and pumping your legs so hard in order to flip yourself over the top of the swing set? Do you remember climbing to the highest limb possible in a tree and then trying to figure out how you would get back down?

When do we stop doing that? When do we become so fearful of dying that we stop living full out?

At some point during an elementary school physical education class, I got hit squarely on the nose with a volleyball. It broke my nose and hurt worse than anything I'd ever experienced. I immediately stopped playing any sport that would involve a ball flying toward me. I always found a way out of it, because I couldn't keep myself from flinching when the ball headed my way and didn't want to come off looking like a "dork."

Then, as I headed into middle school, I drifted into a place of insecurity and invisibility (like most preteen and teenage girls). I wore that cloak of invisibility fiercely. I didn't want to be ignored, but I also wanted to blend into the crowd. Middle school is a rough couple of years that everyone has to go through, survive, and (hopefully) come out stronger on the other end of.

Although I grew through those invisible years, that feeling has reemerged now and then in my career, as a receptionist, as a regional manager of a trucking company, and also during my early years as a Sales Director in Mary Kay. Each time this happened, it was usually Dad who shook me out of it: "You're not living full out, kiddo." Dad would remind me that I couldn't make an impact on my coworkers, my staff, my Mary Kay unit, or *anyone* if I was living invisibly—or hiding in plain sight, as he liked to say.

"Furthermore, what example are you setting for your kids?" he would ask. "Are they going to live life full out, if they see you hiding in plain sight?"

It wasn't until I started speaking for a living that I really let go of the invisibility cloak and stopped hiding in plain sight. I had a passion for my message, and that gave me courage to be powerful and vulnerable at the same time. "There ya go, kid," Dad said. "Now the world can see you."

When my father became terminally infirm, I realized the urgent importance of his words. I didn't want to miss another moment of living with The Colonel. And, I didn't want my children to miss a moment with their Grandpa Ho Ho or miss living full out in their own lives.

We can't have an impact on anyone or anything while wearing a cloak of invisibility. Dying is not a choice. How we live *is*. Don't hide in plain sight. Choose to live full out.

14.

"Just be yourself, kid. Everyone else is taken."

The Colonel said this, or a version of this, to me *so* many times in my life. Each time we were re-stationed to a new Air Force base, there was a new city, a new neighborhood, a new school that I was suddenly thrust into. I had to make new friends and find new groups and new activities. It wasn't easy, but it taught me to get more comfortable in my own skin and become a more reliable friend to *myself*. Each new school held challenges, and it was always tempting to try to fit into the "cool kids" group. Dad would see that struggle—every time. His advice never changed: "Don't try to be the someone you think everyone else expects you to be. When you know who you are, the friends you are supposed to find will naturally gravitate to you."

This advice has served me well throughout my life, although there have been times when I've forgotten it for a while and struggled with my identity. When I stepped away from a public seminar company and first began speaking under my own name and platform, I didn't really know what that platform was or who *I* was as a speaker. Did I need to be Lisa Nichols, or Suze Orman, Jeanne Robertson, or Joyce Meyers? Well, the answer, of course, is none of the above. I needed to be me and develop my voice as I grew in my business and career. Each time I feel a bit off, or out of my element in a situation, I try and remember Dad's wise words.

"You can't be significant if you are trying to be someone else." That someone else was destined to be significant in their unique way. Trying to be them waters down their

significance and delays or defeats who you are intended to be and your own significance.

As Dad would say, "Kiddo, just do you. You're perfect the way you are."

15.

"A title is just that, kid—it's a title. It doesn't define who you are."

During my time in network marketing, I worked very hard to gain new titles and lead each of my team members to new ones. Every time they progressed to a new title, I advanced and received a new title as well. Unfortunately, it's all too easy to feel tied to that title. Lots of goodies and accolades came with every title, and I watched friends and team members gain and lose them over and over, as will happen in direct sales. Each time, I convinced myself that once I earned a position there was no going back. I felt somehow that losing a position or dropping back to a previous title would give me a completely different title: loser. Some months were better than others, and there were months when my position was genuinely in jeopardy. It was during those sobering times that I wasn't having any fun. I was just too focused on potentially losing a title.

Of course, The Colonel always noticed a dip in my spirit and a slow in my step during those times. When that happened, he told me that the title doesn't define my value or how hard I had worked. If I focused only on the title, he said, I'd lose the big picture. Then, he would verbally kick me in the butt and tell me to get over myself—to stop looking at my plight, to stop focusing on myself and go back to concentrating on serving my team.

"Look, kid, there's no problem that a little service to others can't solve. Impact your team, and it'll all come back exponentially."

Titles don't make us who we are. Although we affectionately refer to him as "The Colonel," Dad was a Lt. Colonel at the end of his career. But to many, he might as well have been a Five Star General, because he focused on serving and making an impact. His title didn't matter to him. His purpose did. As a result, his team knew the importance of what they were doing and were willing to work hard beside him regardless of his title.

When we are focused on titles or our standing in an organizational chart, when we are worried about what others are thinking or saying about us, we can't confidently move forward in our life's mission. This prevents us from finding the significance we are destined to attain.

16.

"Be an optimist—always. Perpetual optimism is a force more powerful than doubt and negativity every time."

While I don't know if he ever dreamed of being an astronaut, Dad always felt a particular kinship with NASA, which, in his mind, embodied the power of the human spirit.

I remember so clearly April of 1970 when Apollo 13 took off from Kennedy Space Center carrying James Lovell, Fred Haise, and Jack Swigert. About two days into the mission, the American public became aware that there was a problem on board. Three American astronauts in the void of space, and there was a serious problem on board. An oxygen tank had exploded and blown out a large chunk of the command module.

As a family we watched, we waited, and we followed Walter Cronkite's updates. So many things could go wrong. The crew could run out of oxygen before they reentered the atmosphere. They could run out of water. There could be a toxic build-up of carbon dioxide. There might not be enough power to run the guidance system to get them back to Earth. If they missed their target by a hair's breadth, they would bounce off the Earth's atmosphere and go hurtling into space. The command module might not power up again after being dormant in the frozen void for so many hours. After the explosion and the subsequent cold, the heat shield on the command module could be compromised, which would cause the crew to be overcome upon the reentry. There were so many potential catastrophes that it seemed an impossible task to bring them home alive.

I remember my mother pacing back and forth and saying, "That's it. We've lost three more. We lost three on the launch pad"—referring to the Apollo 1 fire that took the lives of Gus Grissom, Ed White, and Roger Chaffee—"and now we've lost three more."

My father said, "No. We will get them back." Mom ranted about the odds and cried in grief over lives already lost. Dad kept saying, "*No*. We will get them back. This is America, damn it. The best American engineers are on this, and we will find a way to bring them back."

When the command module entered the Earth's atmosphere on its return, there was a standard break in radio communications. I think it was usually about three minutes. To this eight-year-old little girl, it seemed like an eternity. My mother muttered and paced. My father stood stock still, rooted to his spot in front of the television—as if by the sheer force of his will he could make it come out alright. When the sound of Commander Lovell's voice crackled over the airwaves, my father cried. Unabashedly, with tears freely flowing down his cheeks, he said, "You see, I knew we would bring them back. All it takes is ingenuity and will power." (I think this was also the moment that solidified Dad's belief that duct tape can fix anything.)

Is it possible that Dad's optimism, belief, and positive vibes actually helped bring them home safely? Probably not. But the positivity of the NASA engineers looking for solutions they'd never thought of, combined with millions of optimistic and hopeful people across the globe, might have made a cosmic difference. Even in the worst of possible scenarios, optimism will cause you to look for solutions and find options that pessimism will overlook in defeat.

17.

"It's not about what YOU can do, kiddo. That's just vanity. Instead, focus on showing others what WE can do together as a team."

No great thing is ever accomplished entirely alone. Neil Armstrong may have been the first man to walk on the moon, but there were thousands of people working together toward that goal who also could claim the accomplishment. Sir Edmund Hillary may have been the first person to reach the summit of Mount Everest, but he would not have gotten there without his Sherpa Tenzing Norgay and hundreds of team members supporting him through the long climb. No NCAA or NBA championship is won alone, no World Series, and no Super Bowl.

Dad was a huge football fan, and he instilled that passion in me. He believed it was one of the most profound ways to teach life lessons to his daughters. We spent hours in front of the television watching the Dallas Cowboys, Pittsburg Steelers, and Green Bay Packers of the 1970s. On one particular Sunday, as The Colonel was deep into a Cowboys game, he began to school me on the secret to football: teamwork.

"You see Landry in his hat on the sidelines? He spends all week teaching the team how to work together to move the ball and get it in the end zone. He has to use all the people on the team to get it done. The quarterback, Staubaugh, can't move that ball a single yard without his offensive line protecting him. Do you see that receiver, Drew Pearson, there? He has to be ready to catch the pass—every time—whether the ball comes to him or not, he has to be ready. And if that ball is intercepted, they both have to be ready to tackle and bring the defender who intercepted it down.

See the running back? That's Tony Dorsett. He needs to be ready to find the hole to squirt through even before the hand-off comes. That hole isn't gonna happen at all if the offensive line can't find a crack to widen. It doesn't matter what any one of them can do on their own. What matters is how they are ready to support the team at the right moment. And none of them can do anything at all if the defense doesn't do their job when they're on the field. They can only win the game by working together."

So it is in business and our families. No CEO can achieve the mission, vision, and purpose of their organization alone, without the help and support of their managers. Managers need their staff. Spouses need each other, and children need their parents. If we are all just focusing on our own accomplishments and solo efforts to make an impact, we are short-changing the real potential we have when we come together. If we choose to have a *significant* impact, we need to enlist the help of a team and lead them toward a shared goal. This is how we can achieve *and* find significance at the same time—together.

Colonels of Wisdom - Significance

18.

"Focus on who you want to be, kid—not what you want to do. Last time I checked, the Earth is populated with human BEINGs, not human DOINGs."

"What do you want to do when you grow up?" I think every child is asked that question as early as kindergarten. While it's fun to listen to toddlers rattle off a litany of potential careers like fireman, princess, doctor, or superhero, it's probably the wrong question to be asking them. What would happen if we asked a different question instead? "Who do you want to *be* when you grow up?" Furthermore, as children grow, perhaps the question should morph to, "Who do you want to be this year? This week? Today?"

We don't need to wait to "grow up" to *be* the person we are called to be.

As adults, we seem to put so much emphasis on profession and title, when those don't define who we *are*. Regardless of our chosen profession, who we are is far more lasting than what we do. Given precisely the same parameters, no two architects or nurses or software designers are going to create exactly the same end product because each of them is different in who they are, as compared to what they do. Your job function is not nearly as important as what you uniquely bring of yourself to that job.

As a professional speaker, I am always in competition with any number of other speakers who present on my topics of leadership, significance, communication, and conflict management. Each of us brings a uniqueness to the subject. Meeting planners, associations, and corporations book me because they've made a connection with who I am as a person in addition to my areas of expertise. Those who book one of my competitors connect more strongly with who they are.

Our uniqueness, our core values, and the way we view the world will dictate how successful we are and the impact we make on our profession, our coworkers, and our chosen industry.

What you **do** does not define who you **are**. So, when you think about changing careers or starting your first career, don't spend more time thinking about the job function than you do thinking about who you want to **be** within that function.

Colonels of Wisdom - Significance

19.

"Make sure you find a few true friends. We all need someone to cheer us on when we've hit bottom and keep us humble when we get too full of ourselves."

We all need an inner circle. The inner-circle are the ones who are there for you at the drop of a hat and show up even when you didn't know you needed them. They are the ones who always believe in you, while loving you enough to tell you the sometimes-ugly truth right to your face.

It's possible your inner-circle is or includes your family, but it doesn't have to. (Family dynamics are often tricky things!) Sometimes we maintain the same inner-circle for our entire adult lives, but more often than not our circles change. They grow or shrink and morph as we ourselves grow and morph. The best inner-circle relationships are the ones you choose and the ones who also choose you. The Colonel's inner-circle included my Uncle Harry. He was not really my uncle, we just called him that. Harry was always a calm voice of logic and reason for Dad. His circle also included my step-godfather, Lou (my godmother's second husband who we called "Maj"), and Dad's oldest sister, Gloria, who raised him. Regardless of where we were stationed, these were the people Dad would reach out to when he needed to be told a genuine truth.

My current inner-circle includes my husband, who keeps me secure and provides a rudder in my life, and my best friend Diane, who has the biggest heart and most giving spirit I have ever encountered in a human being. My sister, of course, is in the circle. She understands where I come from and makes me laugh loud and cry ugly. Also included is my soul-sister Gracey, who understands the demon that is addiction. She is always there when that demon tries to wiggle its way back into my pores and my life. They chose me—or more importantly, I believe God chose them *for* me. And because each of them knows me at my best and my worst, I know each relationship is *real*. Equally as important, I am there for them when they ask, when they need, and when they don't even know they need me.

Exceptional examples of inner-circles in literature can be found in the dynamic between Sherlock Holmes, Dr. Watson, and Irene Adler, and also in the friendship between Harry, Ron, and Hermione in the *Harry Potter* series. One of the best examples in the celebrity world might be the trust-nugget that is Oprah, her significant other Steadman, and her best friend, Gayle. The primary of each of these example-relationships is better, more influential, and more significant because of the strength, support, and authenticity they draw from those around them.

Throughout your life, you will be surrounded by many people who call you friend, especially if you gain some measure of success, wealth, or fame. Your inner circle should be the ones you *choose*, those few who you allow to see you during the good, the bad, and the ugliest of times. They are the ones who keep you real, honest, and authentic. Without this type of external conscience, it is a near-impossible task to be significant.

You can't be significant alone or in a vacuum of authenticity. Find your inner-circle. Choose people who are loyal enough to always be in your corner and honest enough to be truthful with things you don't want to hear.

20.

"Don't be afraid to make mistakes, kid. They're what make you human, and they're the only way you learn. Failure is not fatal."

Failure is a hard concept for a Colonel's daughter. Disappointing The Colonel was agonizing. Because Dad was the largest and most important presence in my childhood, I wanted to be perfect for him, in everything I did. The "I'm not mad, I'm just disappointed" talk was my worst nightmare. So, it took me well into my adulthood to realize that failure is not fatal. Failure is necessary for growth in any area of our lives.

I imagine most people have heard about Thomas Edison's inventive process and his countless failures while creating the light bulb. It's a valuable lesson in how failure is essential to success. There are many versions of the story of Edison's response when asked about his perceived failure—having made over 1000 attempts before perfecting the process. Two of my favorites are, "I have not failed at all, I have discovered over 1000 ways to *not* create an electric light bulb," and, "I did not fail 1000 times. The Edison light bulb was an invention with 1000 steps."

What would life be like if Thomas Edison had decided to give up at attempt number 750 because he had "failed"? It's hard to imagine very many contributions to society more significant than capturing electricity and making it available to every home and business. Now, I'm a reasonable person, and I know not everything each of us strives for will be as significant as harnessing electricity—but how do we know?

Think about it. What could you do if you took the potential for failure out of the decision? If failing now and then was an acceptable, even expected, part of ultimate success, what would you do differently? Would you strive harder for significance in your work, with your family, and in your community? I think it's worth that paradigm shift. Try it for just a day and see what happens. Try to take the fear of failure out of the equation for the next 24 hours and notice how your actions change.

Colonels of Wisdom - Significance

21.

"You have to have a purpose that drives you forward, something you really believe in. Otherwise all you've got left are your warts to focus on, and that'll kill ya every time."

As a professional speaker, I have a passion for helping my audiences find their own significance and win the battle over drama in the workplace. It is my purpose and my singular focus every time I take the stage.

If I were focused just on being entertaining, or speaking on a topic someone else had chosen for me, I would not be so passionate. I would probably listen more often to naysayers and "haters." Everyone has haters, even motivational speakers. I had one self-defined expert tell me my clothes made me look like a school-marm and I wasn't speaking, I was pontificating. (Great. I am a pontificating school-marm!) Although that stung a lot, if I didn't have a passion, a purpose, and a laser-beam focus on my mission, such a comment would have driven me into a corner to suck my thumb for a year! We are all harder on ourselves than we are on other people, especially when we have been the target of such negativity. If I didn't have an unshakeable commitment to my purpose, I would likely obsess over every hater and tear myself up over every stutter or forgotten phrase.

I've seen this happen to other professional speakers. Those who aren't speaking on a topic they're passionate about tend to be overly concerned about their contract stipulations, their appearance, or their reputation among their peers. They have forgotten their audience and why they began speaking in the first place. Each time that syndrome threatens me, I dig back into the purpose that drives me—to convince the world, one person, one room, one ballroom, or one arena at a time that each person is significant and deserving of respect. If everyone understood that you don't have to respect someone in order to treat them with respect, we could change the world. Focusing on that ideal allows me to move past the moments of doubt and "well-meaning" criticism and continue standing in front of audiences, sharing my message.

Focusing on our purpose, and how that purpose is benefiting others, allows us to accept and look past our own imperfections. Our purpose gives us the strength to be fully vulnerable, human, and, therefore, relatable to those we hope to serve.

Colonels of Wisdom - Significance

22.

"Don't be afraid to shake things up a bit, kid—even if it's just in a small way. You don't have to change the world, but work to change the world around you."

When I was in junior high school, we were stationed at Wright Patterson AFB and living in a Dayton, OH, suburb called Beavercreek. Early in our first year there, I started hearing lunchroom talk about a fantastic opportunity the 8th graders had every year: to go on a canoe trip into Canada with the science teacher, Mr. Hershey. This was a *very* exciting concept for me. It would be something I could do that no one in my family (especially my sister!) had ever done. I could prove my camping and hiking abilities. (I didn't know about rowing so much, but I figured I could learn.) And, I could claim bragging rights as the only member of my family to go to Canada. I was totally on board with the idea!

I heard that the cost of the trip was about $800 for each student, and they only took 12 students each year—so I had to act quickly. Mom and The Colonel agreed it would be a great opportunity, but I would have to earn the money to go. They wouldn't just give it to me. I spent a year taking on extra jobs, babysitting, cleaning neighbors' houses, etc., until I earned the money I needed, plus some extra for spending money on the trip.

On the 14th of January, when registration for the trip opened, I walked triumphantly into Mr. Hershey's classroom with the application filled out and a check for the full amount. Mr. Hershey looked at me a little confused and said, "Oh, I'm sorry, Lauren. This trip is only for boys." I was devastated.

Dejectedly, I shared the news with my parents that night. Mother was outraged. "This is 1974!" she said. "Women can do *anything* men can do and probably do it better. What right do they have to say you can't go?" The Colonel was a bit more even-headed. "We can fight this if you want to, kid. We may not win, but we can certainly shake things up a little. But you need to know that it may make you unpopular with the boys for a while." I didn't care. I had worked hard to earn the money, and I knew I could hold my own with any of those boys around a campfire.

The next day, The Colonel and I walked into the principal's office to state our case. Calmly and clearly, Dad said that mine had been the very first application offered, with payment-in-full, not just the requested deposit. He communicated in no uncertain terms that he was prepared to take this question to the school superintendent and beyond if I was excluded from the trip simply because I was a girl. Over the next hour, a deal was struck. If I could get one more girl to go (so that I had someone to share a two-person tent with), they would arrange for a female chaperone, and I could go.

I had no trouble finding the perfect friend to join us, but we faced the question of raising enough for her payment with only six months before the trip. Knowing the importance of this precedent-setting moment, Dad met with Donna's father and agreed to meet them halfway, putting up $400 for Donna's trip. (I think he probably would have paid the entire fee if he had to, but Donna's folks took care of the other half.)

On the 14th of June 1974, Mrs. Kleibold (the art teacher), Donna, and I joined Mr. Hershey, two other chaperones, and ten boys on a bus headed north from Beavercreek, OH, and we spent two weeks canoeing just north of Basswood Falls, MN. I proved that I could build a rock-lined fire pit better than any of the boys, use a hatchet to splinter kindling off of a log, and build a pretty respectable, long-burning fire. I could portage a canoe, row well, and recover a capsized boat to boot!

The following year, they expanded the trip to offer the opportunity to ten boys and ten girls. Five girls went that year, and the eighth-grade canoe adventure has been at full capacity ever since.

I went back to Beavercreek in 2007. I was speaking in Dayton and had some extra time, so, on a lark, I went driving through my old neighborhood and stopped at the junior high. By providence, it happened to be Mr. Hershey's last year at the school. He was retiring that year.

I said to him, "You probably don't remember, but..."

"Of course, I do, Lauren!" he said, and then he pointed to a framed picture on his classroom wall of me by one of my fire pits.

I didn't change the world by insisting I should be allowed to go on that canoe trip, but we did shake things up a bit in Beavercreek, OH—and maybe made a little bit of progress for women along the way.

23.

"Reset your nose and get back in the game, kiddo. A setback is merely a set up for a comeback."

How many times have you put too many eggs (hopes, dreams, plans) into one basket only to find the basket had a hole in it? I know that has happened to me more times than I care to count. It happens to all of us. The important thing is not to dwell for too long on the fractured eggs, but focus on how you're going to use what's left. Each time I've been faced with what I perceived as a crushing defeat, Dad would remind me of the time he'd broken his nose during a college football game. He didn't want to be pulled out of the game, so he stuck his fingers up his nose in the huddle and reset his nose himself so he could get back in the game.

In November of 1993, a young single mother with an infant girl fled a destructive marriage and arrived on her sister's doorstep, penniless with nothing but a child to feed and the scribblings of an idea for a book in her suitcase. Her mother had recently died as well, and the woman sank into a deep depression, believing herself to be "as poor in spirit, money, and prospects as anyone can be in modern Britain, without being homeless." While surviving on state benefits, she worked away, writing her first novel on her off-hours at the neighborhood coffee shop; taking her daughter there in the stroller would make the baby sleep, and she could write while her daughter slept.

It took her two years to finish the manuscript, which was rejected by twelve separate publishing houses before Bloomsbury picked it up for a modest £4,000—which was not nearly enough to pay her debts. *Harry Potter and the Philosopher's Stone* could have languished in obscurity had the rights to the U.S. publication not been sold at auction to Scholastic Inc. Scholastic bought distribution rights for $105,000, changing the name to *Harry Potter and the Sorcerer's Stone*, and the rest, as they say, is literary history.

J.K. Rowling certainly had her share of setbacks, but she didn't allow them to prevent her from pursuing what she believed she was destined to do. She knew she had something the world wanted, so she reset her nose and got back in the game. She chose to use what was left in the fractured basket she'd been handed to make a tremendous comeback. That comeback included becoming the world's first billionaire author, being named runner-up for Time Magazine's Person of the Year for 2007, and having control of a fantasy empire that spans books, movies, and theme parks. Furthermore, the stories and characters from the *Harry Potter* series are permanently infused in global culture, bringing social, moral, and political lessons to children and adults alike.

Rowling didn't set out with the specific aspiration of being significant. She simply had a burning passion to bring the characters she conceived in her head to life on paper and to create a legacy for her daughter and later children. Transforming her obstacles into new paradigms allowed literature and impact millions of lives globally.

Colonels of Wisdom - Significance

24.

"Happiness is a choice, kid. Choose to be happy where you are, and you'll always be happy."

When I was growing up, we moved a lot. (No really, a *lot*.) Every few years, The Colonel got new orders, and we packed up the house, moved to a new station, and started over. We left behind friendships we'd built, schools and teachers we loved, and states or cities we were used to and relocated to a city or Air Force base where we knew no one at all—often with less than two weeks' notice.

One specific time, we got an assignment to Petersen AFB in Colorado Springs. Dad was going to teach engineering at the Air Force Academy. This was going to be a station we would *love* and one we could stay at for a long time as he would be faculty. We were elated! Well, six months into Dad's tenure at the Academy, he was tapped to head up the Flight Dynamics Laboratory at Wright Patterson AFB in Dayton, OH.

"Great!" Mom said. "I have to go from the Rocky Mountains of Colorado, at the foot of beautiful Pikes Peak to bleak gray skies and cornfields in Ohio. I hate the Midwest!" Later we would make jokes that Mom dug irrigation trenches with her heels all the way to Ohio. As a preteen (and maybe a bit of a drama queen), I picked up on Mom's frustration and saw the whole thing as a punishment. Suddenly I believed my entire existence as a child of the Air Force was a punishment devised to keep me from having a real life.

Dad would have none of it. "You have a good life, kiddo," he said. "This is the way it is, and this is the way it's gonna be. We're going. You can mope about it or choose to be happy about going to an area of the country you've never seen. But one way or the other, we're going. Now get packing."

In hindsight, of course, some of my best childhood memories come from our years in Ohio. I had the opportunity to join Miller's Blackhawks, a world-class marching musical corps, which introduced me to Drum Corps International. That lead to all of my years in marching bands, drum corps, and color guards, which subsequently led to some of the strongest friendships I still hold today. As an adult, I currently live in the Midwest (by choice!) because I remember the magic of the seasons turning and spring flowers.

Relocating every few years could have been a burden for me, but with the right guidance from The Colonel, it allowed me to grow and hone many of the skills (respect, communication, and adaptation) I now teach globally.

Happiness is a choice. In every situation, you can find something to be happy about if you try.

25.

"If you can't see the bright side of a situation, don't give up, kiddo. Start polishing the dull side."

There is a beautiful quote from A.A. Milne's book *Winnie the Pooh*. It is often used or misused on the Internet in memes, but the original goes like this:

> "What day is it?" asked Pooh.
> "It's today," squeaked Piglet.
> "My favorite day," said Pooh.

To me, this is a perfect encapsulation of The Colonel's perspective. Dad was consistently taking something that was broken and fixing it or adapting it into something new. He would see possibilities in what others saw as junk. He kept that same mentality in looking at situations. While the rest of the family moaned and groaned when we got orders to move from the beautiful Rocky Mountains to the Midwest, Dad started looking at all of the places we could visit that were now within a two-day drive of our new station. He talked about growing corn in our backyard and how wonderful it would be to have fresh corn on the cob right out of our garden. He didn't "make the best of a seemingly bad situation," rather, he just stubbornly and persistently *polished* the situation until we could see the good in it.

During my childhood, when my mother would bring out the silver for a special family meal or celebration, it always fell to my sister and me to polish it before we set the table. This was an incredibly tedious task because Mom's silver was quite ornate with lots of little flowers and curly-ques that had to be cleaned with a Q-tip or a toothpick. We hated doing it, but once we were done, it looked so pretty we almost forgot how long it had taken us to get it that way. Just like Mom's silver, once you begin polishing a seemingly bad situation and finding the positives in it, eventually you may just forget why you thought it to be bad in the first place.

I encourage you to look at every negative situation and ask yourself (genuinely, not sarcastically), "What's good about this?" What are the positives in this situation? What lessons can I learn from this moment? How can I use this particular situation to benefit myself and others? If this was the best of all possible scenarios, what would it look like? How can I move it closer to that image? What is one thing I can do right now to make this situation better?

In the cynical world of the 21st century, it's so easy to fall into an Eeyore trap. I do so more often than I care to admit. Like the donkey character from A.A. Milne's book, the Eeyore trap causes people to see only the cloud within the silver lining. When that happens, I have to remind myself of Dad and Piglet and Pooh. Try to polish the edge of that gray cloud and see what the lining looks like.

On any given day, if I can manifest a combination of Piglet's consistent optimism and Pooh's quiet contentment, I think that will make it my favorite day.

Colonels of Wisdom - Significance

26.

"Your attitude determines your altitude."

While I now know this quote originally came from Zig Ziglar, The Colonel was the first person I ever heard it from, and for 40 years of my life, I thought it was entirely his wisdom. Regardless of who said it first, it is a certainty. And, in Dad's house, a positive attitude was non-negotiable.

I've never met, nor have I ever heard of, anyone who is wildly successful with a consistently negative attitude. Your attitude, whether positive or negative, is always "leaking" out of you in some way. The question to ask yourself is: "What am I leaking? Is it fresh, positive and fragrant, or is it stale, negative and skunky?" The reality is that you can do everything wrong with a positive attitude and still succeed. The best example of that comes from the cinema: Forrest Gump. That entire movie is an homage to the fact that you can do everything wrong in life with a great attitude and still succeed. On the other end of the spectrum, though, you can do everything perfectly to policy with a stinky attitude and get nowhere.

We have all met people who light up the whole room when they walk in. As I travel and speak, I see it consistently. These positive people come into the conference room or arena and others smile and wave, offering up the seat next to them. Usually, these bright lights have many offers to choose from.

We have also encountered people who suck the very light and life from the room. These people are great black holes of negativity, consuming any and all optimism in their wake. As these people enter the arena, they are spotted peripherally, and suddenly everyone else becomes profoundly focused on their conference schedule or workbook. I see them casually pick up their purse, coat, or briefcase and set it in the seat next to them to indicate that it's unavailable. You cannot be impacted by or have an impact on people that refuse to be around you.

While every cloud has a silver lining, actually seeing that silver lining is a choice. It may surprise you to discover that positive people don't always wake up with a positive attitude. Some mornings I wake up and say, "Good morning, God!" Other mornings I wake up and say, "Oh good God, it's morning."

When you can't immediately see the silver lining, create one. My husband, Ron, has a characteristic phrase that works when nothing else will: "That beats a poke in the eye with a sharp stick!" I'm not sure if he was consistently threatened with sharp sticks as a child or what, but, in his book, anything and everything beats a poke in the eye with one. Therefore, to him, anything that is not a poke in the eye with a sharp stick *is* a silver lining. Realistically, for most of us, were we to take a serious look at our lives in comparison to others across the globe, we would see how very blessed we are.

Maintaining a positive attitude in our inherently negative world is not necessarily easy, which is why we must be ever vigilant. A positive attitude is a choice. When you discipline yourself to make it a daily choice, it becomes a habit. So, I encourage you to look at every moment and ask yourself if it beats a poke in the eye with a sharp stick! Because your attitude does, indeed, determine your altitude.

27.

"Mind your attitude, young lady. If it's not an attitude of gratitude it'll trip you up every time."

There's an ancient Persian proverb that says, "I cursed the fact I had no shoes until I saw a man who had no feet." I spend a lot of time talking about the importance of a positive attitude and how Dad made it an imperative in our household. The reality is that a solid attitude has to be about more than just positivity. It also has to be heavily steeped in gratitude.

While there is a plethora of research on the physical, psychological, and emotional benefits of gratitude, I don't believe Dad had read any of it. This is something The Colonel just knew instinctively. Being consistently grateful helps you enjoy the good moments in your life and gives you strength to deal with the bad moments. It helps you build stronger relationships and maintain positivity in a negative situation. No one's life is perfect, and yet there is always something to be grateful for. Everyone has to deal with adversity, complaints, burdens, betrayals, and obstacles. Still, when we discipline ourselves to look through a lens of gratitude consistently, we are more able to see the flickers of goodness in our lives. Furthermore, focusing on gratitude allows us to recognize the large and small gifts we have been given by our parents, our friends, our neighbors, our employers, and our Creator. It helps us maintain a necessary humility.

When I was at a particularly dark moment in my life and aggressively rebuffing all Dad's attempts to paint a silver lining for me, The Colonel gave me an assignment. It had been many years since Dad had issued me an "order," but some obedience habits never change. Dad's task was to begin a gratitude journal. "Go get yourself a spiral notebook and, for the next month, every night before you go to bed, write down three things you're grateful for. No dittos, kid. Each night has to be unique." I will admit, initially it was a struggle, and I didn't always manage three. There were some days during that first month that the best I could possibly write was, "At the end of this immeasurably horrific day, I am grateful that I'm still alive." But being disciplined in carrying out Dad's assignment (which I have continued off and on since) allowed me to see how very blessed I really was and begin to find the glimmers of hope in what I had previously perceived as a hopeless situation.

Finally, I believe an attitude of gratitude allows us the emotional space to give to others. Mary Teresa Bojaxhiu, most commonly known as Mother Teresa, often talked about how grateful she was to the sick and dying in the slums of Calcutta. She said being grateful to those unfortunate people God had placed in her path allowed her to deepen her faith and give more to them than she ever thought possible.

What would happen in your world if you focused on being grateful? When we are thankful for what we have been given, we are more willing to give to others, and that is a path to significance.

28.

*"Stumbling block or stepping stone —
it's your choice, kid."*

Everyone encounters obstacles in their lives. It's the obstacles, not the opportunities, that build our character and make us resilient. There have been so many times I stumbled in my life and my career—and each time, The Colonel would pick me up and dust me off emotionally and then tell me I had a choice. It was my choice to let it (whatever the "it" of the moment was) stop me or to use it as a reason to keep pushing forward.

The most recent of these conversations came in my head in its entirety after Dad had passed. I had established my original speaking business brand and built my message on a particular phrase that I used often. That phrase was the foundation of everything I taught. When I consulted an intellectual property attorney about a trademark, he told me that it was too common a phrase and I would never get a trademark approved, so I didn't try. Nine years later, I was speaking at a conference with another speaker who had a brand *very* similar to mine (not identical, but centered around that common phrase). A week after I returned from that conference, I received a "Cease and Desist" letter from his attorney. My colleague had actually obtained a trademark for that very common phrase six months after I had inquired about it initially. I was devastated. I stormed and steamed about it for a while, but there was no getting around it. He had the legal right to use the phrase, and I did not. It wasn't his fault he had a better lawyer than I did.

As obstacles go, this was a big one. I was branded entirely with this phrase (which I am not sharing here out of respect to my colleague). All of my marketing materials, my website, my demo-video, my brochures—*everything* had that phrase on it, and I was now legally prohibited from using it. I thought my business was through. I wanted to curl up in a corner and suck my thumb. That's when Dad's voice crept into my consciousness.

"Stumbling block or stepping stone—it's your choice, kid. Are you gonna let this stop you from speaking? Are you gonna let this stop you from delivering a message you feel so passionately about?"

Suddenly I realized that I didn't have to change any of my message; all I needed to change was how I worded the message. I replaced the common phrase with one I use now and continue to deliver globally. I then had to also find a new brand, which any branding expert will tell you is no simple task. Yet, processing this very formidable obstacle brought me to the real and genuine brand that wholly encapsulates who I am and what I teach: The Colonel's Daughter.

Making the transition was expensive and time-consuming, but a year after I launched *The Colonel's Daughter* brand, my business had doubled and has continued to grow exponentially since. I attribute that growth to the fact that the presenter (me), the brand, and the message are genuine and now in complete alignment. This molehill of an obstacle had become a mountain of a stepping stone.

What are the molehills in your life? How can you reevaluate your situation to look at them as stepping stones instead?

29.

"Don't take yourself too seriously, kiddo. Truth is, if you take yourself too seriously, no one else will."

In his time, my father was quite influential in the research and development of aircraft and ordinances. Without a doubt, his ideas and the teams he led shaped the trajectory for the future of the United States Air Force. When he called, people took his call. When he spoke, people listened. His insights and wisdom were taken very seriously. Nonetheless, The Colonel never took himself too seriously.

Dad was a master at making light of himself. When I was little, Dad would drool his food on purpose, while seeming to instruct me on proper table etiquette. It made Mom crazy. When the movie *Airplane* came out in 1980, Dad spent a good six months throwing water on himself and saying he had a "drinking problem."

The first time I remember The Colonel expressing this particular life lesson, I was nine years old. Dad had made special arrangements to take me to a Father-Daughter Ball at the Officer's Club on the Air Force base. I had never actually been *inside* the Officer's Club. I was there every day in the summertime, but only at the pool and the snack bar. Children were not allowed inside. It was a very formal and mysterious place to me, so I was very nervous and excited. Mom had threatened me about being on my best behavior and not embarrassing my father. Dad decided to take me to dinner in the formal dining room before the ball. I was dressed in my favorite blue velvet dress and The Colonel (although he was not a Colonel then, but a Major) was in his dress uniform. I felt so important when we walked up to the Maître D, who looked up before my father spoke and said, "Major Leigh. We have your table ready. Right this way, please."

Dad rarely shared small talk with us. He was usually educating us about one thing or another. That evening, somehow the conversation ended up on wing configuration and how the different shapes of airfoils changed the way a plane flies—different shapes for different purposes. To best explain his point, he excused himself for a moment and came back with three or four pieces of paper, which he started folding into paper airplanes of various shapes and wing sizes. When he had finished folding, he asked me which one I thought would fly the farthest and the straightest. I pointed to one, and he said, "Well, let's just see."

Then he tossed the paper airplanes, each in a different direction across the formal dining room of the Officer's Club. This created quite a rumble of muttering, which exploded into a downright ruckus when one of the planes crashed nose-first into an older woman's soup! It splashed all over her sparkly dress. The Maître D tried to calm the woman and offered to pay for her dry cleaning. Then he came over to us and suggested we finish our meal in the private dining room. I was mortified, certain that Mom would be furious with me. Seeing the look on my face, Dad said, "Oh, don't take yourself too seriously, kiddo. If you do—no one else will." Then Dad tipped his hat to the soup-splattered woman and grinned from ear to ear. "Just wait until it gets around to your Mom that I got kicked out of the Officer's Club dining room for crashing a plane into Mrs. General Stewart's bouillabaisse!" Then he laughed so hard he snorted, and we laughed all the way to the private dining room where we finished our dinner.

When you are doing significant work with others who hold you in high regard and pay attention to you, it can be all too easy to internalize that attention and begin building puffed-up self-importance. That might even be a natural response. The problem is that when you start to take yourself too seriously, others stop doing so. When you believe yourself to be too significant, you become less so.

30.

"Like a small pebble makes a ripple, even a very small action can have huge significance."

In 1981, a woman fled her abusive husband, not knowing where she would go or if she would even make the escape successfully. Her husband was a long-tenured police officer with political connections throughout the state. She knew if she didn't leave, she would die. She also knew that if he caught her, she was determined to end her own life before he could. It was one last desperate attempt to break free. She left with nothing but the clothes on her back and drove to a town across the state line. She abandoned her car in a lake and walked to a McDonald's about a mile away. There she sat for hours, trying to figure out her next move (or if it was even worth continuing on) when a stranger approached her. The elderly stranger placed a bag containing a hamburger and fries in front of her, saying, "Forgive me for presuming, but you looked hungry," then walked away. Inside the bag, on top of the napkins, was a card that simply read "Safe House" along with an address. After a few more hours, the restaurant was closing, so she asked at the counter for directions to the street named on the card and then walked for three hours to find the address. Knowing it could be a trap, but not sure what else to do at three in the morning, she took a leap of faith and knocked on the door. The nondescript home in a quiet neighborhood was indeed a shelter for battered women. There she found compassion, security, therapy, and the resources she needed to move across the country to Phoenix, AZ, making a fresh start under a new name.

A decade later, this same woman, my friend Theresa (not her real name), was serving as the executive director of a non-profit that maintains a collection of nondescript safe houses in quiet neighborhoods around the Phoenix area. I was with her for support as she stood before a closed session of the city council of a Phoenix-area suburb. She told her story and asked for the use of an abandoned store front currently owned by the city. She proposed building something that had never existed before, a one-stop location with all the services and resources necessary for a battered woman to break free. She received her approval and began implementing her plan. There was no ribbon cutting and no fanfare when the one-stop opened its doors a year later. From the street, it was an unassuming clothing boutique storefront. But here, a woman who might be being followed could walk in and never be seen again. In a separate space inside, volunteers are always standing by. Police officers who are personally vetted by Theresa herself, given her history, are ready to take a victim's statement. Doctors wait to care for and assess physical harm. Therapists are there to evaluate psychological damage and begin the healing process. There are children's counselors if a victim has brought her children with her, and, most importantly, an unmarked, average looking car is waiting outside the back door with a driver ready to take the victim through a back alley to a shelter. Over the past 20 years, this unremarkable storefront has been a portal to freedom for thousands of women in Arizona.

When Theresa was healing and recovering in the original shelter, she asked about the older woman who had given her the bag that night in McDonald's. No one knew who she was. The shelter has volunteers come in periodically, and they always have a stack of the cards available for volunteers and supporters to take, should they see someone who might need help. No one could put their finger on who that one woman might have been.

It was a small action the older woman took. She could have read the situation completely wrong, but she did it anyway. The unknown woman's small action had a ripple effect that changed my friend Theresa's entire life and helped thousands of women as a result.

31.

"Activate your brain before you engage your mouth. You will never know who your words are influencing."

I can't remember the first time Dad said that to me, he said it so often. I tend to be a talker. When curious people ask me how I got into the speaking profession, I tell them that for my entire life people have been telling me to stop talking! In college, I studied non-profit public relations and theater. In public relations, you really have to think before you speak so you are representing your client in the best possible light.

In the mid-1990s, I was the managing director and public relations voice for the largest community theater in the state of Arizona. We had functioned for decades in a quaint little barn that sat on 2.5 acres. Through a complicated set of circumstances beyond our control, the 2.5 acres were sold at auction to a very powerful and well connected executive in the Phoenix area. He then arranged to resell it at a profit to a retail business who wanted immediate occupancy. There was only one little hiccup—the theater. We had a binding lease on the barn for the next 11 months. You can't just pick up and move a theater with a season ticket base of thirteen hundred. The season had already been sold to capacity, and season ticket holders had already selected their favorite seats in the existing configuration. Scene designers had already submitted plans for the season's sets based upon the current space. All in all, it was a terrifying prospect that threatened to put us out of business.

Negotiations began, and the theater turned to the city, which had been asking us to move into the downtown area for some time. We thought it was a perfect opportunity for the city to put their money where their mouth was and provide us use of available space downtown. A week before we were to go before the city council with our proposal, the artistic director and I were having lunch in a local restaurant to discuss our strategy. Not being known for his calm demeanor, the artistic director became agitated and a bit loud, saying, "Well, [the mayor] isn't gonna do us any favors. She's in [the executive's] pocket. He says jump, and she asks how high?! She's not gonna do anything to jeopardize her gravy train!" I responded that this was conjecture on his part, but, if that was the case, we needed to figure out how to sway the rest of the city council. A moment later, a woman who had her back to me in the booth behind me stood up to leave, and I watched all the color drain out of my colleague's face as the mayor walked past us to leave. "Well, now we're royally screwed," he said.

Unfortunately, he was right. The city council voted down our proposal unanimously. Would we have gotten the city council votes had the mayor not heard our conversation? There is no way to know. But, I *am* confident the conversation resulted in her swaying the rest of the council against us.

As it turned out, we fought a lengthy legal battle (which we couldn't afford) with the executive's corporate attorneys and managed to stay in the space until the very last day of our lease. This allowed us time to secure a space in a neighboring city. That difficult battle and inevitable drop in season ticket holders nearly put the theater under, but it has been resilient, growing each year since then. Twenty-four years later, the theater is the centerpiece of the neighboring city's newly built performing arts center and thriving downtown area.

When I began my speaking career, The Colonel felt it important to reiterate this sentiment to me. "Now you are speaking to arenas full of people who are there to hear your wisdom and your insights. Feed them only the best. You never know when some off-hand comment from the stage that you forget about the next day will stick with someone for life. You will never know who your words are influencing." I take this very seriously, and I repeat it to all of my audiences when speaking on communication. If you think there is any possibility that what you are about to say might be construed as offensive to anyone within earshot (not just the person you are speaking to), don't say it. We've all had those, "well, I probably shouldn't say this, but..." moments. If you think you shouldn't say it, don't.

Activate your brain before you engage your mouth.

32.

"If you focus on being a mirror to someone, showing them how wonderful they are, their mirror will inevitably turn back toward you."

Some people are drawn naturally to the spotlight. Others are not. Those of us who thrive on stage with a microphone in our hand and spotlight on our face are accustomed to people telling us (either sincerely or at a shallow level) how wonderful we are. If we start to believe that of ourselves, we become less and less relevant. Please don't misunderstand me; there is value in self-confidence and knowing you have a valuable message to impart. Unfortunately, when the goal becomes showing others how wonderful you are, you lose your message and become just more noise in the universe.

For the past 14 years, I have been fortunate to have a secret weapon. She doesn't know she's my secret weapon, but she is. Like Popeye had his spinach and He-Man had the power of Grayskull, I have her. When I am down and questioning myself, she lifts me up. But she is *most* valuable to me when I start thinking I'm "all that." I meet with my secret weapon as often as my schedule allows, but I make a rule that it's no less often than once a month.

Because I know it's all too easy for me to focus on myself and what I have going on (especially when I am feeling rather braggadocios), I try to discipline myself to begin every visit asking about her. As she catches me up on the various facets of her life, work, and family, she reveals the beauty of her soul and the most profoundly giving spirit I have ever encountered. I am in awe of it and am gently humbled by its presence every time I'm around her.

For some strange reason, she thinks I am amazing, and being with her always makes me feel better about myself as a human. She makes me want to be more and better than I am. She does that naturally, without thinking. It's a special and unique gift she has, so I work hard to focus the mirrors in my eyes on her, so she can see how amazing *she* is and how drab my life would be without her.

Everyone has someone who makes them feel special. How wonderful would it be if you would focus the mirrors in your eyes entirely on them? Allow them to see themselves through your eyes. What a simple, cost-free, but highly significant gift that would be!

33.

"Unless you're on the battlefield, no one is ever going to give you a medal for doing what is right. That doesn't mean you should stop doing what is right. Every decision has consequences."

My definition of integrity is not mine originally; it came from that great philosopher, Anonymous. Integrity is doing what is right because it's right—every time—whether anyone is looking or not. It's that last clause that is the sticky part. Every day we are faced with moments, big and small, when decisions have to be made with integrity. The "no one will ever know" or "no one is looking" moments are the trickiest.

Now, two decades into the 21st century, it's unrealistic to believe that no one is watching, in some way, from some angle. Between satellites, traffic cameras, security cameras, cell phones, and smart devices, one would be hard-pressed to find a space that's not under some sort of surveillance twenty-four hours a day, seven days a week. In the metropolitan area where I live, there was a scandal involving a superstar running back (RB) for the local NFL team. The RB was accused of brutally hitting and kicking a woman at a hotel. The RB told the team owner and executives that it never happened and she was just making up a story to extort money out of him. That lasted until the video from the hotel hallway was obtained. The video showed the woman taunting and verbally abusing the RB—and then it showed, very clearly, the RB hitting and kicking her several times and leaving her lying there in the hallway. The RB was cut by the team, not so much because he had done the deed, but because he had lied about it and now could (in the team owner's mind) never be trusted again.

Even if you find yourself in the remotest region of outer Mongolia, hundreds of meters down a tightly spaced cave that is accessed only by a blow-hole on top of a mountain, with no electronics or technology within a thousand miles—someone is always watching. If you believe in a higher power, regardless of what form that higher power takes, that higher power is watching.

Even if you *don't* believe in a higher power, someone is watching and that someone is perhaps the most important: your subconscious. Our subconscious is the most powerful critic and judge in the universe. When we do something that we know is wrong, even if no one else could possibly have seen it, guilt creeps in at some level. Guilt robs you of your self-esteem. Even if it is a thread of guilt no thicker than half a hair on your head, that niggling little thread worms its way into your subconscious and sets about destroying your self-esteem.

It happens to all of us. It's happened to me more often than I care to remember, in big decisions and small ones. Each time, I have had to backtrack and make amends to lop the guilt off at its source and begin rebuilding my self-esteem. It happens to all of us because we're all human, and we make mistakes. That is why it's so essential to make an effort every day to do what is right because it's right—every time—whether anyone is looking or not.

34.

"It's not just about impacting lives. Hitler impacted lives. It's about *how* you impact them. That's a choice you have to make every day, kiddo."

There is an obscure gothic romance novel I read once that told the story of two brothers, each born of the same impoverished family. While gothic romance novels usually serve the purpose of providing a few hours of fluff reading (and this is why I like them now and then), this one offered a more profound lesson for me.

Through the complicated machinations that often exist in these novels, each brother built himself up to a position of wealth and power through separate means. The older brother, Edwyrd, grew to manhood bitter and spiteful against all the things he believed he'd been deprived of as a child, taking careful note of each perceived slight and insult, each hardship and deprivation. The younger brother, Alwyn, saw the world through different eyes. He took careful note of each of those who had helped him, sheltered him, and those who had even less than he had.

Edwyrd used the wealth and power he gained in adulthood to gather to himself all that he believed he deserved after he had been so sorely abused in his adolescence. He hoarded his wealth, cheated those below him in stature, and contrived to punish anyone he believed had ever wronged him. Alwyn used his position to assist and support those with lesser means and to repay debts to all those who had cared for and supported him throughout his youth.

Not all gothic romances end well. In fact, many end with someone in anguish throwing themselves off a jagged cliff! This one ended, as one would expect, with the death of both brothers. Edwyrd died wretched and alone, having driven away everyone in his life, a lonely phantom in a cavernous mansion of dust-gathering opulence. Alwyn also died of old age, but in a cozy country estate, surrounded by a loving family and attendants who were determined to continue his good work and maintain his legacy.

Those few hours of fluff-reading and the deeper lesson this novel offered have stayed with me all these years. It reminded me of The Colonel's primary belief that how we impact people is a choice.

Whether you are in a support position, leadership, or customer service, how you influence people, whether positively or negatively, is a daily choice. Especially if you are in a public or quasi-public position such as clergy, entertainment, or politics, how you impact people must be a discipline. Are you, by your actions and with your words, hoarding, controlling, demeaning, or dismissive? Or are you supporting, empowering, and encouraging others to believe in themselves?

If your life were written into a novel, would your behaviors and words cast you as Edwyrd or as Alwyn?

Colonels of Wisdom - Significance

35.

"You can't antagonize and influence at the same time, kid. One will always undercut the other."

It is normal and natural to be influenced by people you like, and it is possible to be influenced by those who you revere or admire but don't necessarily have an affection for. It is nearly impossible, however, to be influenced in any positive manner by someone who is antagonistic toward you.

On stage, I often tell the story of a sales manager at the van line who invited me into his office to share a seven-page list of all the things I do (did) that irritated him. "Lauren," he said, "let me put this in terms so simple even you can understand." He intended that I should change each one of the irritants immediately if I wanted to keep my position. I learned a great deal that day, but it was not from the sales manager. I went home from that meeting and did what any good Colonel's daughter would do: I called Daddy to whine. The lessons I pulled from that day came from my father, not from the sales manager.

The Colonel encouraged me to rise above those petty, dismissive comments. He challenged me to improve my communication with the sales manager and to make sure my backside was always covered. He encouraged me to double my efforts in support of the sales staff and make them look good so that they could shine even under the thumb of a poor manager. And, he challenged me to do my job to the best of my ability, so I could more quickly be transferred to a different department. (As it turned out, shortly after that, I was promoted to a position that was a management peer on the organizational chart, and the sales manager lost his job completely.

... I had nothing to do with that.)

There is a plethora of examples in sports, entertainment, and politics of people who choose the path of antagonizing or denigrating their rivals, or even their supporters. Inevitably they will lose those supporters and be bested by their opponents. Choose to emulate those who build people up, not tear them down. If you want to be in a position of influence and help guide people's thinking or policy, the route to doing so is never to be abusive, antagonizing, or dismissive. The only path to positively influencing people is compassion, empathy, and empowerment.

36.

"When you know what you want your legacy to be, you will naturally behave in a manner that builds that legacy."

One of the things Dad repeated to me often was, "What you do speaks so loudly I can't hear what you say." Like so many of his quotes and sayings, it was not original to him. I've subsequently seen it attributed to Zig Ziglar as well as at least a dozen philosophers dating back to Confucius. Still, Dad is the first person I ever heard it from. It comes to mind here because just saying "this is what I want my legacy to be" is meaningless unless you proactively do the things that will create that legacy. I could easily *say* I want my legacy to be that I was the greatest ingenue in Broadway history. Unfortunately, although that might have been a dream of mine when I was much younger, having never performed on Broadway, that dream legacy is never going to happen.

Many people ramble through their lives without determining what they want their legacy to be. There is nothing wrong with that; it merely leaves the definition of one's legacy to others. To be genuinely significant, though, I believe you must decide how you want others to remember you and set about making those memories a reality. Deciding what impact you want to leave on the world is crucial to bringing it about. Why would you leave that to chance?

My sister is a remarkable human being. She has a Ph.D. in Chemical Engineering and has spent her entire career working on containing nuclear and other toxic waste and abating their effect on the environment. That is vital and admirable work to be sure, but it's a job. It's not what she wants her legacy to be. In addition to that critical work, my sister breeds championship dogs. Her breed of choice is the rare-breed, Belgian herding dog. My sister has produced and championed these beautiful dogs for two decades and can claim the number one dog in the country three times. She decided very early on that she wanted to be known as the owner, kennel, and breeder who created the most durable pedigree line in America for her breed. She runs her kennel the right way, without crossing any gray lines, and she desires to be a deep well of information about the breed she loves so much. To that end, she diligently chooses and approves anyone who buys one of her puppies. She controls and co-owns her dogs that exemplify the model of the breed and carefully selects who those dogs are bred with. As a result, her program is considered a gold-standard in the AKC (American Kennel Club) and a model for ethical breeding practices.

This didn't happen by accident. It took hard work, long sleepless nights in the whelping room, and some aggravation when others she partnered with wanted to cut corners. It would have been much easier and more lucrative for her to have farmed her dogs out for a fee or sold her puppies to the highest bidder, but that would not have been what's best for the dogs, the breed, or her legacy.

What do you want your legacy to be? What are the actions that will bring about that legacy? What are the acts, errors, or missteps that could prevent that legacy from coming to fruition? Defining these things now allows you to be proactive. It enables you to measure everything you do or say against the standard of "will this help or hinder my legacy?" so that you can then make decisions accordingly.

37.

"Prejudice is intentional ignorance. You have to be bigger than that."

I was having a casual conversation with a colleague recently. We were both awaiting flights to different locations and, by chance, had run into each other in the layover city. (This happens more often than you would think in my industry.) He was recounting an exchange with one of his audience members that had rattled him that day. He ended his thought with, "This obsessive 'cultural correctness' these days... I just think it's stupid." I don't know him that well and was not eager to get into a tussle were I to challenge him on that mindset, so I let it be and moved on to a safer topic: football. Still, I was saddened because this colleague speaks on the subject of leadership.

I believe, and share in nearly every one of my sessions, that our goal as leaders and communicators is to allow all people to feel safe (physically, intellectually, and emotionally) and treated with respect in our presence, while we stand our own ground and get our message across. If that is the case, then this "obsessive cultural correctness" is not stupid; it is imperative. How can I endeavor to help someone feel safe and treated with respect in my presence if I am blindly or naïvely repeating something that might be construed as offensive to them? A casual response to that would be, "Well, how am I supposed to know what might be offensive to someone? I can't know everything!" While it's true we can't know everything, I believe it's our responsibility to know as much as we can.

The Colonel was adamant about this. He believed that prejudice is intentional ignorance. If you never allow yourself to learn or understand a paradigm different from yours, you prevent yourself from being significant. You prevent yourself from having an impact on anyone who doesn't think or believe *exactly* as you do.

Dictionary.com defines prejudice as:
> *"Unreasonable feelings, opinions, or attitudes, especially of a hostile nature, regarding a racial, religious, or national group."*

I would agree with that, and go beyond. My definition of prejudice is any negative feeling toward anyone who looks, thinks, believes, behaves, speaks, dresses, smells, moves, or functions differently than I do. That is, any negative feelings toward anyone who is different *because* they are different. Prejudice is not something inherent in us at birth. Small children don't shy away from playing with someone because they look or sound different. Small children are not afraid to ask the simple, often blunt questions that will help them to understand. Prejudice is taught and molded into children by their parents.

We all have prejudices whether we are willing to admit it or not. The question then becomes, are we willing to live comfortably in those prejudices or are we willing to get uncomfortable and learn about something different than ourselves? You may not understand someone's beliefs, their sexual identity, their cultural norms, or their life experiences coming from a different life environment than you do. Still, you limit yourself by not trying to understand, by not seeking insight, by not asking questions. To dismiss something, or worse, someone, because you have no common frame of reference is to make yourself small, through your ignorance in choosing not to investigate. So, ask questions. Endeavor to learn about something you don't understand. Build a common ground wherein "cultural correctness" comes naturally. You grow automatically when you have an openness toward learning what is acceptable and what might be construed as offensive to someone else.

You can't be significant and close-minded. The two are mutually exclusive.

38.

"The only way you can impact anyone is to understand them a little bit.
Ya gotta be able to see through someone else's eyes, kid."

My life's journey has taught me beyond a shadow of a doubt that there are three sides to every story: yours, mine, and the truth. Each person views life, love, conflict, work, justice, and faith from their own paradigm. Each person's unique, personal journey shapes their perception. Therefore, I can't ever truly see things from your perspective, nor can you ever truly see things from mine. Still, I can try to put myself in your shoes long enough to empathize with your position.

According to WordNet by Princeton University, "empathy" is:
> *"the capability to share your feelings and understand another's emotion and feelings. It is often characterized as the ability to 'put oneself into another's shoes.'"*

Empathy, therefore, comes from a commonality, a oneness. It involves the ability to understand how a person is feeling based upon a similar experience. It pertains to the ability to say, "I can imagine how that feels." While I may have never placed my hand on a hot stove and received third degree burns on my hand, I've tripped and fallen against the furnace in our home and received third-degree burns on my arm. I can, therefore, say, "I know how that feels." I may not have watched my spouse or child in the prime of their life waste away and succumb to the ravages of cancer, but I have watched my late mother do so. I know the sickening feeling of helplessness and the sad sense of loss. I can, therefore, empathize.

When my children were young, my family took a vacation where we drove in a large loop across eight states. We spent two weeks piled inside our land-yacht Cadillac, driving no more than 300 miles in a day. We stopped to see anything and everything we wanted to see. It was one of the most fulfilling and memorable experiences we've had as a family. One of the stops we made during that trip was outside Rapid City, SD. We went to see Mount Rushmore, as neither the kids nor I had ever seen it. It is an awe inspiring sight—an engineering and artistic marvel. At that time, there was a newly remodeled visitor center, and patriotic music played all along the American flag-lined walk up to the viewing platform. It is a national monument that genuinely does what it is supposed to do: stir raw emotions of patriotism in the hearts of Americans.

The next day we went to see a different monument, the one being forged out of a mountainside not far from Rushmore to honor the Oglala Lakota Sioux Chief Crazy Horse. A tour of *that* visitor center leaves you with a very different feeling.

My first impression was something along the lines of, "Gee, they haven't gotten very far with this thing, have they?" Then I read the information in *their* visitor center that noted the project has firmly rejected federal funding, which might have moved the monument along at a faster pace. They have steadfastly refused assistance from a government that, as they see it, has never kept one promise it ever made to the Sioux Nation. Reading the story of

Crazy Horse and the sovereign people he represented, one gets a very different sense of the history so stirringly chronicled just a few miles away at Mount Rushmore.

Leaving the Rapid City area, I was deeply troubled by the dichotomy of our history. I thought of Dad and my mother often saying, "Walk a mile in their moccasins, Lauren Ann." If some nation or group of people decided today, in the 21st century, that America was a land of promise and wealth and that they were, therefore, going to take it for their own—by force—we would fight to the death to defend our homes and families from the occupying power. The thought of someone walking into my house and saying that it is theirs now, simply because they want it and have the force to take it, is absurd to us in today's reality. Yet that is precisely what happened on this continent some 200 years ago. The English, the French, and the Spanish each carved out a piece of this continent with no regard to the sovereign nations that were already here.

Sadly, even as I contemplated that, I was struck with the futility of any empathy I might pretend to feel within the context of *my* life. What happened to the Native Americans, the indigenous people of this continent, was wrong. We would not stand for such a thing today.

It was *wrong*. Yet here I am, 200 plus years later, and what can I do about such an injustice? If someone was to come to me and say, "You are right. It was wrong. Therefore, we're going to give it all back to the Native Americans, so pack your things and get out." I would say, "Oh, I don't think so. This is *my* home. I bought it. It's mine." America was their home first. It is my home now. There are three sides to every story: yours, mine, and the truth. If I can't personally fix it, then the best I can do is empathize.

The only way to genuinely empathize with another person and get at the truth of any matter is to try to see things through their eyes, to walk for a while in their moccasins. We may not be entirely successful in doing so, and it's not always a comfortable journey. Still, it's an excellent place to start. It's also the only path to impacting that person.

39.

"You can't be present unless you're present, kiddo."

I attended elementary school on two Air Force bases. There are a few things that were different about attending school on base. Sometimes, the lesson would be interrupted about once an hour by the roar of jets flying overhead. (Such a fantastic sound. You can't understand if you didn't grow up with it, but it is oddly calming.) Other times we would have to be escorted home for our safety when the Vietnam War protests got too close to the school. But the thing that sticks out the strongest in my memory, to this day, is the process of roll call. On an Air Force base, there was only one acceptable response when your name was called: "Present, sir" or "Present, ma'am."

Once, after attending a parent-teacher conference, The Colonel sat me down to have a chat. "Mr. Perry says that you are consistently distracted in class, your mind wanders, and you doodle. Is that so?"

"Yes, sir. I'm sorry."

"Kiddo, you can't be present unless you're present. Being physically present is just not enough. You can't learn anything if you're not paying attention." Unfortunately, we had to have this conversation more than once, as I have mild ADD and am always chasing squirrels in my brain.

In the 21st century, Dad's admonishment is more relevant than ever before. According to research published in *Psychology Today*, our minds are accustomed to processing an average of 120 images per minute and creating between 69 and 97 random thoughts per minute. With advancements in smart technology, there is no time in the day or night when we can't be connected unless we consciously decide to unplug. So, it is easier than ever to be physically present without being present in the moment.

Recently, I was standing at O'Hare airport, checking on my gate. I was not in the middle of traffic, but far enough out in the walkway that I could see the departure board. I looked to my right just in time to see Mr. Jr. Executive with his slim-cut silk suit and his expensive haircut, his face fully planted in his cell phone, on a direct trajectory to hit me. There was no time for evasion. I planted my feet and took the charge—full force into my right side. The Venti latte he was carrying succumbed to inertia, flying out of his hand past me and exploding as it hit the floor with a splatter pattern away from me.

He apologized, as he helped me up off the floor. "Geez! I'm sorry, I was distracted."

"I see that," I replied. "Remind me to never get in a car with you," I said to his back as he strode away with his face back in his phone, leaving the spilled coffee and cup where it had landed.

While a decade or two ago I would have been unnerved by someone checking their cell phone in the middle of one of my keynotes, it's a common practice now. I know that many people take notes on their phones or tablets, and I am more than happy to have someone tweet out a quote from me. I do that often when listening to a colleague speak.

But there are times when it is vitally important to be in the moment. Having a one-on-one with a member of your team, hearing about your child's day or your spouse's day, or having lunch with a friend are all times when it's essential to be in the moment. There are thousands of missed opportunities every day because we're so "connected" that we're disconnected from being present.

Significance requires knowing when to disconnect from the data-stream and be engaged in the moment with someone. It requires an ability to look someone in the eye and process the meaning behind the words they're saying to you. It requires disciplining yourself to turn your device off, put it away, or leave it in your car so you can be fully present with someone.

You can't be present unless you're present.

40.

"You don't have to be rich to be giving. Sometimes a simple 'thank you' to someone will be the most memorable gift they receive that day."

When you grow up in the Air Force and relocate every few years, it's often hard to maintain relationships with distant family members. There was the core—The Colonel, Mom, Christi, and me. The four of us were the only blood family I had a relationship with for a long time. Living in that reality allows you the option of *choosing* your "extended family." My godmother, Sara, was part of my chosen extended family. Now, to be truthful, Sara was not really my godmother. She was not the distant relative who stood with my parents when I was baptized as an infant. I don't remember meeting those godparents, and I can't even remember their names. I call Sara godmother because she functioned in that role for me. A godmother is one who steps in when your parents aren't around—one who guides you, who supports you when you've done something stupid and have to learn a hard lesson from it. Sara was all of that for me.

Every time we were stationed at Kirtland AFB in Albuquerque, NM, Sara was there also. The first time, her husband was also stationed there, working with Dad, and the last time she and Lou had retired there. When Mom was buried in her alcoholism and incapable of parenting and Dad was on TDY (temporary duty) away from home, there was Sara. It seems like I was always at Sara's house.

Sara had a habit that I didn't realize I had also picked up until well into my adult life. The last thing she would say to someone upon concluding a conversation, almost every time, was, "I appreciate you." Sara said people didn't offer appreciation to each other nearly often enough, so every chance she got, she let them know they were appreciated. "No one really *has* to do anything for me, Lauren Ann. So, when they do, I think it's important to let them know I appreciate it while I still have the opportunity."

I believe Sara felt the fleeting of time more than many. Her first husband, Tommy, was piloting an F-4 Phantom that was shot down over Laos when I was six. His remains were never recovered. After several years, she fell in love with Tommy's best friend, Lou. Six months after we celebrated their wedding, Lou was deployed. He was shot down and imprisoned at the "Hanoi Hilton" for four months. When he came home, he was never quite the same. Time took on a significant importance for Sara. Perhaps she thought that if she didn't express her appreciation today, they possibly might not be here tomorrow. So, she took every chance she got to let the people around her know they were appreciated.

We lost Sara in 2011, and I try to keep her example alive. When I am conversing with a speakers bureau who has booked me or is trying to get me scheduled, I let them know that their efforts are appreciated. When I am working with a customer service agent to get an issue resolved for me, I tell them I appreciate them and their time. Sometimes a simple thank you is enough, and sometimes it's important to go a small extra step to say explicitly, "I appreciate you."

Who do you interact with daily who makes your day or your job easier? It's possible that helping you out is their job, but we all know a job can be done well or it can be done in a shabby manner. A job can be done cheerfully or begrudgingly. When it is their job, and they do it well or cheerfully, or they go above and beyond—let them know they are appreciated. Say, "Thank you." Say, "I appreciate you."

41.

"Pay attention, kiddo. You may be hearing, but you're not listening. That's not gonna get you anywhere with anyone."

I was sitting in the Dallas/Fort Worth International Airport recently on the last leg of a very long trip home when I observed a mother traveling with two small children. The little girl was probably about five, and the boy was just beginning to walk. We were both waiting to board for a 9:30 p.m. departure, and it was apparent to me that the mom was worn out from negotiating airplanes and airports with these two small children. The adorable five-year-old was prattling on and on about something very important to her, while Mom was trying to allow her toddler son to get his energy out and still keep him somewhat confined. I found myself overwhelmed with empathy for this woman, thinking to myself, "I have no idea how I would manage if I had two little ones to keep track of all on my own in an airport."

I was just about to turn my attention to other people watching when the little girl did something that struck me as profound. She reached up and captured her mom's face between her two chubby little hands and said, "Mommy, listen to me—and this time, listen with your eyes." Wow. That innocent but profound sentiment brought me back to The Colonel, telling me to pay attention.

How often do we find ourselves engrossed in the chaos or even the minutiae of the moment, and we let our minds wander? We completely forget to listen with our eyes—we forget to listen *actively*?

It's equally as common to find ourselves listening with the intent to respond, scripting our "Yes, and…" or "Yes, but…" in our heads before the other person has even finished their sentence. You can't be significant if people feel dismissed or glossed over when they are talking to you. Active, empathetic listening involves turning off the chaos and the internal dialogue and focusing entirely on what the other person is trying to communicate to you.

In business, as in life, we automatically feel a bias toward people who we believe are listening to us. We also feel an unconscious prejudice against people who we think are not listening to us. We want that bias in our favor! One of the most valuable significance skills we can possess is the ability to set aside our own agenda long enough to genuinely listen to someone else's. This, more often than not, allows you to hear the message behind the words and more fully understand them and what they are feeling.

Long-term significance requires the ability to listen actively. So, next time you are listening to someone, turn off your internal dialogue—and don't forget to listen with your eyes.

42.

"Don't focus on what you aren't. Focus on what you ARE and how you can use that to get where you want to be."

Colonels of Wisdom - Significance

"Comparison-itis" is an insidious disease. It is especially damaging in both the direct sales world and the professional speaking world, the two industries I have spent the past 24 years of my life in. But let's be honest, it's horrible in any arena of life. Chances are pretty good that in your life or career you have encountered someone you admired and might have been a tad bit envious of. When you compare yourself to them, it's natural to come up short in your own eyes and feel miserable because of it. Sometimes, the result of that is trying to duplicate what they've done, only better—which rarely works in your favor either.

For me, this disease first reared its ugly head at home. My sister is the smartest, most accomplished woman I know. She worked hard and excelled at *everything*. Every quarter, my parents would post both of our report cards on the refrigerator—hers with a big smiley face on it and mine with "You can do better!" scrawled across it.

It wasn't until I was in treatment for my bulimia that I finally gave voice to the monster that was "comparison-itis." My sister was so good at everything she did, and I couldn't see how I could possibly measure up. "*That* is the problem," The Colonel pointed out to me. He said, "It's not a competition! Stop trying to be your sister. Stop trying to duplicate her efforts." Dad told me that my job was to figure out my own strengths and use those to make my unique path in the world, not follow her path. "*Don't focus on what you aren't,"* he said. *"Focus on what you ARE and how you can use that to get where you want to be."*

Fortunately, my sister and I have different skill sets, each very valuable to the world. As soon as I found those qualities that made me unique and useful, I was able to stop comparing myself to my sister. Furthermore, as we have grown as adults, my skills have proven valuable in shoring up areas that she is less adept in, and I actually help her out now and then.

That doesn't mean I don't still compare myself with others who are seemingly more successful, more competent, more accomplished than I am. I do. We all do. The challenge (and the reason why this disease is so insidious) is that when we compare ourselves with other people, we automatically compare our weaknesses to their strengths. We lose that comparison every time. Why would you do that to yourself? I try only to compare myself with my own best efforts. Then I can focus on improving upon those best efforts.

You can't be significant if you are trying to be someone else. You have a unique combination of gifts and abilities, and comparing yourself to someone else prevents you from using those abilities that are uniquely yours. Stop comparing.

43.

"Sometimes ya gotta walk through fire to prove who you are. You've been through more than anyone should have to, kid. Prove you're bigger than all of it."

Sometimes it's easy to get caught up in our own "stuff," isn't it? Everyone has "stuff." No one gets through life without some adversity. I believe it's how we deal with the adversity that defines us. Some of Dad's quotes listed in these books were things he said so often they are ingrained in my mind by repetition. This one, however, came at a specific moment when time slowed to a crawl, like slow motion in a movie. That particular moment was when I truly understood the difference between reaction and response.

Reaction is emotional. It's visceral, or knee-jerk. Response requires thought—and often, a *lot* of willpower. In all of life's situations, it behooves us to respond rather than react.

I am a woman of the Me-Too movement. I have experienced sexual harassment hundreds of times and survived sexual assault twice in my life. I am a victor, not a victim. I have long since done the hard work required to process through the emotional garbage an assailant leaves behind. Doing so is like walking through a cesspool, hoping you'll find a way to climb out and wash off. But on that particular night, frozen in my memory, I was not yet out of the cesspool. It was immediately after the last assault (the details of which are immaterial for this narrative), and I was twenty-two years old.

After the assault, and once I got myself home, I should have called 911.

I should have, but I didn't. A profound sense of shame completely crushed me. How could this have happened to me *again?* It surely *must*, therefore, have been my fault for being out at two o'clock in the morning, broken down on a freeway wearing nothing but dance clothes and flip flops with no contingency plan.

I never called the police. The police would have asked questions I couldn't have answered like, "Why was I out so late after dance rehearsal in nothing but dance clothes?" "Why was I driving a car on its last legs?" "Why hadn't I taken better care of my car so I wouldn't be in that situation?" "Why had I not gotten a license plate number or a good look at the man?" "What did I expect them to do about it now if I had nothing to give them to go on?" I didn't call the police. Instead, I called my father.

Dad was furious with me for not having called the police. He was utterly unequipped to deal with such emotional wreckage from 500 miles away, so he did what he did best, he kicked into survival mode. He told me to go to the doctor and get checked out. He analyzed what had happened to my car, and, based on my description of how it had broken down, he decided the engine was fried. He arranged for a rental car until I could get another vehicle.

Then he told me that how I responded to this would define who I am for the rest of my life.

"Sometimes ya gotta walk through fire to prove who you are. You've been through more than anyone should have to, kid. Prove you're bigger than all of it."

My life's journey has taught me beyond a shadow of a doubt that what happens to you in your life is not as important as how you choose to *respond* to what happens to you in your life. It happened to me. It was horrible. I survived. It didn't break me. I am bigger than all of it.

We all have "stuff." It's your choice whether that stuff breaks you or makes you stronger, giving you the foundation you need to be empathetic with others as they go through *their* stuff. Use your stuff to the benefit of others.

Prove you're bigger than all of it.

44.

"Your goals shouldn't focus on what you can achieve for yourself. Instead, they should only serve as markers, measuring the progress you make in pursuing something greater than yourself."

Dad was obsessed with being of service. If I set my mind to doing something, he would only assist or offer advice to me if it had a service component. How was this thing I wanted to do or have going to help someone other than me? As I grew older, the expectation was that my accomplishments must include opportunities for others in my sphere to achieve something *they* wanted as well.

During my tenure with Mary Kay, I learned that personal accomplishment would only take me so far. To move into management, a consultant has to help other people achieve their goals. As a Sales Director, my focus couldn't just be on hitting production goals (which couldn't be achieved alone), but instead, it had to be on helping the entire unit achieve their individual, personal goals—one consultant at a time. While my Director friends and I would make jokes about figuring out whose backside we could "shove up the ladder of success" in order to achieve our own goals, it was just in jest.

There were times, I'll admit, that I tried to do it alone with maximum personal achievement for my unit. All that accomplished was my devoted unit members sitting down and watching the "Lauren Schieffer Show," and the unit didn't grow. Directors with longevity understand the privilege of serving their unit, listening to each team member to learn more about her goals and the *why* behind those goals, then providing the opportunity to stretch and grow. It's only with their success that a Director achieves her own success. In turn, because that success is born out of service, it is a way to attain significance as well.

You don't have to be in direct sales, lead a team, or grow up in the military to pursue a goal larger than yourself. Every city and small town has a food pantry that needs to be stocked, a homeless shelter that needs compassionate volunteers, a playground yet to be built, a school that needs a fresh coat of paint, or a community fishing pond that needs tending. The opportunities for service abound. All you have to do is look around you. Choose something today that resonates with you and shift your focus from you and your achievements to working in collaboration with your neighbors, pursuing something that will benefit others—something greater than yourself.

45.

"You were born for a reason, kiddo. Everyone is. Most people aren't self-aware enough to figure out what that reason is."

Although Dad did not believe in organized religion, he did believe in a larger, universal design. "The world just works too well to believe it's all by chance," he said. He felt that no human being is a mistake, every person was born for a reason, and it is tragic if someone dies not knowing what that reason is. Unfortunately, I believe that happens all too often. If we are not encouraged to examine what our purpose is (the reason we were born), we could ramble through life without ever discovering it.

I have a friend from my theater days who moved to New York "to make it big and become a household name." All of his friends, me included, believed he would achieve his dream. He was talented and charismatic, disciplined and level-headed. He rattled around off-Broadway for a while, waiting for the big break to happen. When his money ran out, he started directing on a freelance basis. That led him to accept a job directing a musical for a retirement community. We spoke right after he accepted the job. "Well, it's not gonna make me a household name," he said, "but it's a paycheck."

We talked again a few weeks after the show finished, and I asked how it had gone. "Oh, it was great!" he said. "We are already planning the next one. It was so much fun and so rewarding to see how much joy this brings to everyone —those in the show and those watching it." Ten years later, my friend has created a non-profit organization that stages musicals in retirement homes across the country. He's not a household name, but he genuinely believes this is what all his theater background was leading him to and feels wholly fulfilled in this endeavor. He has found his purpose.

If we aren't specifically encouraged to pursue finding our purpose, we might miss out on it entirely. Fortunately, there is wisdom available to help one discover their purpose. There are books and workbooks. (I have one available, as do others.) There are guides and coaches (Some worth the money, and some not so much.)

But, before investing in books or coaches, I recommend doing some personal self-searching on your own. List your accomplishments, large and small, then identify both the aptitudes and the abilities you utilized to achieve them. You will begin to see patterns develop. Then, make a listing of things that bring you contentment, the feeling that all is right with the world, and things that bring you joy, a feeling you know will not last but are thrilled to experience in the moment.

If you truly invest some time in personal self-searching, and don't just gloss over it quickly, I believe you will be well positioned to figure out the reason you're here. Furthermore, if you then decide to spend funds on books, workbooks, or coaches to delve more deeply into the subject, you will be in a better position to utilize the information and guidance effectively.

You were born for a reason. Don't ramble through life, not knowing what it is.

46.

"You can't be significant riding on the coattails of someone else's values."

You can be very successful and make a lot of money without ever defining what you value and what (if anything) you would be willing to die for, but you can't be significant without knowing what your core values are.

Whether we are conscious of it or not, our values are formed in us practically from birth, and they color the way we see life, love, work, relationships, ethics, recreation—everything. Truly understanding what your core values are offers you a rationale for *why* you do what you do. Your values provide a rudder that guides you and a foundation that stabilizes you when life's seas get rough.

It is vital to keep your core values in mind to guide you when you need to make important decisions about life, work, love, etc. I had a conversation with my neighbor late last year that reminded me of how important this is. She was struggling internally with her travel schedule and asked me how I handle mine. I suggested that our situations are very different. She has three small children at home; mine are grown. "When you were in my workshop two years ago," I said, "you identified one of your core values as family. When did that change?"

"It didn't," she said. "I took this Regional Vice President job *for* my kids. With the extra income, I can provide so much more for them than I could before."

"And yet," I said, "with traveling now three weeks out of every month, that promotion has taken you away from one of your core values—your family. That might be one of the reasons you are hating the travel so much."

If you value something, it will play a prominent part in your daily life.

I highly recommend you do some sort of exercise to evaluate your core values at least once a year, because often they change. What we value in our twenties may be very different from what we value in our forties or our sixties. There is a plethora of systems on the market designed to help you define your values, some more in-depth than others. Find one that works for you and use it regularly.

Knowing, living, and working according to your core values allows you the freedom to function within those values and beliefs, which contributes to your self-esteem and your peace of mind. Furthermore, knowing your core values will enable you to make decisions in serving and benefitting others, while keeping in alignment with those values.

Colonels of Wisdom - Significance

47.

"Don't worry about making grand gestures, kiddo. It's the little things, done consistently, that create significance."

I have a friend who I will call Barbara. When Barbara and I were in college, in the marching band together, she started putting aside money for what she called a "Little Fund." She had heard about a clarinet player from her high school who could not attend the solo and ensemble competition because her instrument had broken. The school did not have a clarinet to loan her, and her family could not afford to get hers fixed right then. So, this promising musician missed the solo and ensemble contest in her senior year of high school. This weighed heavily on Barbara's heart, so while most college students were using their wages to eat out or (more likely) party, Barbara started setting aside a percentage of her paycheck from the campus book store for her Little Fund.

The following year, Barbara reached out to all the high schools in the area to let them know that, if a student needed assistance to buy, rent, or repair an instrument, she could help. That year she helped two students who otherwise would not have been able to participate in their high school band program.

Barbara and I have remained friends since college. She graduated with a medical degree and is a practicing surgeon, but she maintained her love of music and plays in a civic orchestra. All the while, she has continued to stash the same percentage of her income toward her Little Fund to help student musicians. The difference, of course, is that her income has grown tremendously. Last year Barbara was able to buy instruments for two high schools in underprivileged areas *and* offer scholarships to ten students across the country who want to study music but would otherwise be unable to afford advanced education.

Barbara does not advertise or make a big deal about her philanthropic efforts. Some years she gives more than others. You can't apply for her assistance. She has a tight spiderweb of music-educator confidants who help her identify potential needs and sift through the best candidates. Her only stipulation, from the very beginning, is that she remain anonymous.

Barbara did not set out to change the world, and she doesn't make grand gestures in her giving. She has simply done one thing consistently over time. Because of her Little Fund and her passion for music education, music is flourishing in areas where it might otherwise not have.

What little thing could you do consistently that would make a difference in someone's world?

48.

"Don't let the silly little dramas of each day get you down. Stay positive, and when you're surrounded by negativity, you can rise above it."

I am a news addict. I admit it. I inherited it from both of my parents. I also wear my heart, my head, and my tongue on my sleeve. So, this particular wisdom from The Colonel has always been very hard for me. I have to put extra effort into not letting the negativity in the world pile on me.

At least since the beginning of the 21st century, and probably before, what passes for "news" is increasingly sensationalism masked as news. Unfortunately, the good news is rarely sensational, so what sells is usually the negative stuff. Add politics to that sad reality, and what spills out of newspapers, your television, and the Internet is a smelly swamp-sludge of rotting negativity. So, the answer would be not to watch, listen, read, or pay any attention to the news. Unfortunately, just like those who know smoking is bad for them, but continue to smoke anyway, being a news junkie is an addiction. It comes with a dreadful fear of missing an essential story or piece of data that will allow the whole world to suddenly make sense.

If someone is weighed down by negative news as they begin their day, that negativity can start to snowball. The snowball grows when they get into a petty argument with a coworker. After work, they step in a puddle, and on their way to their car, they trip on a shoelace and land face-first on the pavement. While filling their tank at the mini-mart, they spill gasoline on themselves, and when they get home, their spouse berates them about forgetting to feed the cat before they left in the morning. Their snowball is now the size of a small Volkswagen. In the mail, they find a written nasty-gram from their homeowners association fining them for leaving their trash can by the side of the house instead of in the garage, and suddenly this Volkswagen-sized snowball takes them crashing off a cliff. Any one of these smallish things would be easy to overcome emotionally, but the combination of them all can become overwhelming. Without the right emotional armor, a buildup of tiny annoyances could send a person under for good.

That is why it's so important to discipline yourself on positivity daily. I know my days are *always* better when I don't start them with the news. I admit I'm not capable at this point of going a whole weekend without knowing what's going on in the world, but I'm always better when I don't start with it. Also, I don't recommend ending your day with the news, right before trying to sleep.

I also have affirmations that I repeat to myself when I start to go down a negative path. ("This is not about me. Stop taking it personally." "They are not angry at me. They are angry at the situation." "I am not in control here, but God is, so I am content." And so forth.) These keep me on the sunny side of the street.

Thirdly, I always try to shift the focus off of myself and how I am feeling and transition my attention to someone else and how I can brighten their day. I have found it nearly impossible to remain negative when I am focusing on bringing emotional sunshine to someone else.

There will always be negativity in the world. There will always be day-to-day annoyances, and sometimes lots of them will gang up on you. Discipline yourself to do what is necessary to rise above the harmful sludge of negativity and stay on the sunny side—both for yourself and for others.

49.

"Significance grows out of inspiration and empowerment, not out of intimidation or domination."

It is human nature to be inspired by someone who is doing something you also want to do—especially when they are doing it for the right reasons. (The right reasons, as I see it, would be for the good of others or the community, as compared to what is explicitly going to benefit you. Sometimes both happen, and that is a delightful result, but the former should always outweigh the latter.) There is nothing wrong with wanting to be an inspiration, but there is only one way to go about it. Inspiring someone requires leading by example in the right direction for the right reasons. That has a far more lasting impact than imposing your will on someone to force them in a particular direction.

Empowering someone is a different challenge. Inspiring someone to go a certain direction is important, but if you don't also enable them with the tools, skills, and confidence they need, the inspiration is short-lived.

Intimidation and domination are the opposite of empowerment.

This adverse motivation can be cloaked in many ways. Pushing, compelling, or forcing action upon someone is the opposite of empowering them to do something. That may create short-term results, but it will also breed long term resentments. Micromanaging someone's efforts is also not empowering them. Instead, that implies a lack of faith in their abilities and will also breed lasting resentment.

Empower someone by asking them open-ended questions, which allows them to create their own path in the direction they're inspired to go. Make queries that don't undermine their decisions, but challenge them to think through and validate their choices. Give them the tools and support they need and ask for, without the implication that they cannot succeed without you. Be a guide and a mentor, not a director or a taskmaster.

By virtue of his size, my father could have dominated any conversation, room, or decision had he chosen to, just by sheer force. He rarely made that choice, though. He knew from experience that every time his temper or frustration got the better of him, and he forced his will by brute strength, someone ended up hurt, either physically or emotionally. So, he worked consciously to make different decisions and forge different paths. Dad knew that significance and influence came from inspiration and empowerment, not from intimidation or domination.

To make a significant impact, you need to strike a delicate balance. Endeavor to lead by example in the direction you believe others should go, and then empower them with tools, guidance, and the belief that they can succeed in that direction. This creates a legacy because it shows them how to have a significant impact as well.

50.

"Pay attention to the moment. The moment is everything."

Throughout my youth, my family owned a plot of land on a lake in southwest Colorado. These eleven acres with a rustic A-frame cabin (which we built ourselves) were the only constant in a continually shifting world for me. Regardless of where we were stationed, we always went "home for the summer" to spend weeks at the cabin. There are thousands of moments burned into my memory from the cabin, but this one specific moment stands out.

It was evening, after dinner, and The Colonel had built one of his massive bonfires. (Dad built a fire pit large enough to roast a whole pig or three dozen steaks at one time. Naturally, because he had a massive fire pit, it required an equally enormous fire.) Dad was stretched out fireside on a folding lounge chair, and I was curled up under his arm. I asked him what we were going to do the next day. *"I don't know. I really don't care, kiddo. I'm enjoying this moment right now. Pay attention to the moment. The moment is everything."* And then he asked me about my day and listened as I recounted every meandering path I'd taken through the woods and every flower I had found in the meadow. There was no grand gesture in that moment, no money spent, no speeches made. It was just a quiet moment between a father and his daughter that made her feel valued.

I believe significance is found in the small moments. Unfortunately, with our 21st-century pace, it is all too easy to miss the opportunity to make someone feel valued by just taking a moment. When a co-worker stops by your desk, take the time to pause. Look them in the eye and ask them a question focused on them. How are they doing? How was their weekend? What did they think about the game last night? Did their child make the team? Take the time to listen, and then pay attention to their answers. Make them feel valued.

Maybe there is a community charity you volunteer for. If that work brings you in contact with those who benefit from the charity, take a moment. Look them in the eye. Who are they? How are they? What can you do or say to make them feel valued?

One of my clients is a nursing home in the Midwest. I am continually amazed and blessed to watch simple exchanges that happen between the staff, the residents, and their families. There are no grand gestures, just simple little moments. The moment when a nurse, dietician, or social worker takes the time to look a resident in the eye and listen to what they have to say is profound. When staff takes time to be patient when someone aging forgets where they were in a conversation or repeats themselves, it's a moment. When the social worker allows the time for a family member to process through the emotion of handing over the care of their loved one to someone else, it matters.

How many small moments pass us by without notice because we are focused on what we perceive as more pressing things—what we deem to be more important? Whether it is at home, at work, in your place of worship, or in your community, the small moments are opportunities to make others feel valued. Pay attention to the moment. Take a moment. The moment is everything.

51.

"There is goodness and beauty everywhere, kid—even in things that seem scary or ugly. Look for the good. Look for the beauty and the fear or hatred will melt away."

I have an irrational fear of spiders. Really—pictures of spiders in a magazine will send me across the room. I am okay with just about any bug, lizards, snakes, etc., but if it has eight legs and walks sideways, in my opinion, it is a minion of the devil and deserves to die. Once when I was about ten and we were in the process of building the cabin in Colorado, I encountered a wolf spider in the large tent the whole family slept in. I refused to go back into the tent until Dad killed the spider. He told me I was being silly, and it wouldn't hurt me if I left it alone. Nope. No way. Either I occupy the tent, or the spider does, but not both together at the same time. It just wasn't gonna happen. Dad squashed the spider, and only once I watched him remove the eight-legged corpse from the tent would I go back in.

Early the following morning, Dad took me around to the site of where the cabin was going up. He had something he wanted to show me. As the sun came over the top of Engineer Peak, the first rays landed on a massive spider web spun between two skinny pine trees. This web was easily twenty inches across and had microscopic droplets of dew hanging from it that caught and reflected the early morning rays. It took my breath away, and I started to step closer to it when I noticed that the web was occupied. I instinctively took three steps back. Dad nudged me forward again and said, "No kiddo, don't look at the spider. Look at the web. Take a good look at it. Look at how delicate and perfectly it's formed. Each strand is meticulously woven together to create this beautiful web—and all of that happened overnight, because it wasn't there last night when we were working over here." I said, "It really is pretty." "Yes, it is," he responded. "And this thing of beauty came from something you find scary and ugly."

When my daughter was just about two and we were up at the cabin, she took a stroll with her Grandpa Ho Ho to see what they could find. She had her arm raised high over her head so she could grasp the large, calloused finger my dad held out for her. I followed at a distance with the camera. They stopped in a meadow to examine a dandelion. I thought to myself that Dad would share a story about my making dandelion flower wreaths for my hair when I was little, but what he plucked for her was a dandelion that had gone to seed. I thought, "Well, that one isn't very pretty, is it?" She blew the seeds away and erupted in joyous laughter. She came running back to me, "Did you see? Did you see, Mommy? All the feathers blew away! It was like fireworks!" It was so eye-opening. This pesky weed that we dig out of our perfectly sculpted lawns, in its final death throes, became beautiful and sparked delight in the eyes of a little girl.

I wish I could tell you that Dad's little spider web lesson cured me of my fear of spiders. It didn't, not in the least. And, I am not going to say that moment with my dad and my daughter caused me to allow dandelions to grow in our lawn. I don't. But I do remember the moments, and I always try to find something beautiful or meaningful in things that cause me fear and anger.

I acknowledge there are people and situations in the world that should rightly make us angry or afraid, but mostly what we fear or think we hate are things or people we don't understand. What would happen if you disciplined yourself to genuinely work at finding the good in a bad situation? What if you tried to find beauty in everything you see and encounter? Even if you can't find good and beauty in *everything*, trying to do so will allow you to find it in things you would never previously have believed you could.

52.

"Control what you can. Let go of what you can't."

I confess. I am a recovering control freak. I've found this is something that's never cured, only managed. (I would have said only controlled, but the control freak trying to control her need to control is a rabbit hole I choose not to go down.) I've learned from experience that trying to control everything in your life, work, relationships, and environment leads to stress, physical ailments, and paralysis of action. So, it's essential to assess what you can control and release everything else.

When we were building that cabin in southwestern Colorado, there was an enormous, ancient ponderosa pine that stood about 20 yards from where the back door would eventually be. Mom loved all trees and was loathe to remove any of them in the construction process, but Dad knew the old pine was losing its integrity and would come down eventually on its own, potentially right on top of the cabin. "Control what you can," he said. This was something he knew he could control—when and how that tree came down. So, he dug into the skills he'd learned in his late teens as a lumberjack. He climbed high in the tree to secure guidelines to manage what direction it would come down. Christi and I each had a rope. It was our job to keep the tension on our lines, and when we heard the tell-tale crack that said the tree had snapped, pull as hard as we could, and then get out of the way. Slowly and methodically from the top down, Dad cut pieces of the old pine off so that felling it would not damage the partially built cabin, the meadow, or the surrounding pines. Taking the one, old pine down was something he knew he could control to protect the cabin from damage.

During my last year of high school, a wildfire erupted in Colorado that threatened the lake and our property. From our home in New Mexico, Dad spoke with the emergency response coordinator, giving them permission to clear some trees, building a firebreak on our land. I asked him, "Aren't we gonna go up there, Dad?"

"Nope. We'd only be in the way. This is out of my control. I've done what I can, and I've got to let the rest go."

I was angry. "So, we're just gonna let it burn?!" I said.

"Honey," he replied, "you've got to control what you can and let go of what you can't. If it all burns, it all burns. The trees will grow back, and we'll rebuild the cabin. Either way, it's out of our hands, so it's no use gnashing your teeth about it."

This has been a hard lesson for me for my entire life. My current voice of reason is my husband. He has an amazing ability to let go of that which he can't control and not take it on internally. During the Great Recession of 2008, I became anxious and agitated about the retirement funds we had worked so hard to build simply vaporizing with the stock market. (I say we worked hard. It was really *his* hard work and consistent saving that had put us in a good position to retire early—until 2008.) Ron consistently reminded me that it was totally out of our control, and therefore, it was not worth getting aggravated. Of course, I fussed and fumed anyway. (As I said, it's something I have to work on consistently.)

As hard a lesson as it might be for me, and maybe for you, it's a crucial one. Whether it's business, politics, pandemics, economics, or choices made by others, it's not beneficial to get worked up about things you can't control. Genuinely significant people understand what they can control and what they can't. They put their energy into managing those things they can, toward the best outcome for all involved. Pumping energy toward trying to control things we can't control, and getting frustrated or angry about such things, saps the effort that could be better channeled elsewhere—toward something you can control.

Acknowledgments

All praise, honor and glory go to my Father in Heaven who is bigger, stronger, wiser, and more patient even than The Colonel and who crafted me for a specific purpose.

Thank you, **Ron Schieffer**, for always being willing to proofread my work before I send it to an editor. And for doing it (for the most part) on my time schedule. I know you would rather just sit and let your brain relax. I appreciate and love you more than I can ever express.

Thank you to **Lindy Rosenson**, for your initial help and ideas for this volume.

Thank you, **Diane Schmit**, for being my secret weapon.

Colonels of Wisdom - Significance

The Colonel and my daughter discover dandelions together.

ABOUT THE AUTHOR

As the daughter of a career Air Force officer, Lauren Schieffer, CSP, gained a profound independence and ability to adapt to changing circumstances with grace and humor. She shares lessons learned from "The Colonel" and 20 years in business with corporations, associations, and not-for-profits across the globe.

Able to relate to and energize everyone from custodial staff to the C-suite, Lauren is a master storyteller, delivering insightful and relevant content that empowers people to absorb and act upon what they've heard—and she does so with a dry sense of humor that keeps them chuckling while they're learning.

Her enthusiasm is infectious and her passion unmistakable.

Made in the USA
Columbia, SC
28 December 2022